POCKET

SIEM REAP &
THE TEMPLES OF ANGKOR

TOP SIGHTS · LOCAL EXPERIENCES

NICK RAY

Contents

Plan Your Trip

Banteay Srei (p117) ZZVET/GETTY IMAGES ©

Welcome to Siem Reap & the Temples of Angkor

Siem Reap is the life-support system for the temples of Angkor – eighth wonder of the world – and a regional hotspot for wining and dining, shopping and schmoozing. Angkor is a place to be savoured, not rushed, and Siem Reap is the perfect base from which to plan your adventures.

Angkor Wat (p82)
©DANNY JACOB ©2012 ©

Top Sights

Angkor Wat

The eighth wonder of the world. **p82**

SIPPAKORN/SHUTTERSTOCK ©

Angkor Thom & Bayon

The enigmatic faces of the Avalokiteshvara. **p92**

Ta Prohm & the Small Circuit

The ultimate Indiana Jones fantasy. **p104**

Floating Villages of Tonlé Sap

Waterworld on the great lake. **p138**

Beng Mealea

A slumbering giant in the jungle. **p130**

Banteay Srei

The art gallery of Angkor. **p117**

FAR LEFT: JASON LANGLEY/GETTY IMAGES ©; URF/GETTY IMAGES ©

FAR LEFT: PIER GIORGIO CARLONI/SHUTTERSTOCK ©; MARISHA_SL/SHUTTERSTOCK ©

Preah Khan

A fusion temple of Buddhism and Hinduism. **p111**

Phnom Kulen

The holy mountain of Mahendraparvata. **p122**

Koh Ker
A remote rival capital. **p126**

Siem Reap Activities
Adventures beyond the temples.
p32

FAR RIGHT: TIM GERARD BARKER/GETTY IMAGES © LLUIS CASTANEDA INC/GETTY IMAGES ©

FAR RIGHT: TIBOR BOGNAR/ALAMY STOCK PHOTO © KEVIN YULIANTO/GETTY IMAGES ©

Roluos Temples
The early capital of Angkor. **p135**

Angkor National Museum
A showcase of Angkorian art.
p30

Eating

Unlike the culinary colossi that are its neighbours Thailand and Vietnam, Cambodia is not that well known in international food circles. But Cambodian cuisine is also quite special, with a great variety of national dishes, some drawing on the cuisine of its neighbours, but all with a unique Cambodian twist.

The Staples

Freshwater fish forms a huge part of the Cambodian diet thanks to the natural phenomenon of Tonlé Sap lake. They come in every shape and size, from the giant Mekong catfish to tiny whitebait. Rice and *prahoc* – a fermented fish paste that your nose will soon recognise at a hundred paces – form the backbone of Khmer cuisine.

Cambodia in a Bowl

For the taste of Cambodia in a bowl, try the local *kyteow,* a rice-noodle soup that will keep you going all day. Don't like noodles? Then try the *bobor* (rice porridge), a national institution, for breakfast, lunch and dinner, and best sampled with some fresh fish and a splash of ginger.

Unidentified Frying Objects

The fiercely omnivorous Cambodians find nothing strange in eating insects, algae, offal or fish bladders. They will dine on a duck foetus, brew up some brains or snack on some spiders. They will peel live frogs to grill on a barbecue or down wine infused with snake to increase their virility. To the Khmers there is nothing 'strange' about anything that will sustain the body.

Best Khmer Fine Dining

Chanrey Tree Designer restaurant on the riverside offering contemporary Khmer cuisine. (p58)

Cuisine Wat Damnak Seasonal set menus are a sensation at this renowned restaurant. (p66)

Mahob Super-stylish restaurant that offers more than just the 'food' the name suggests. (p59)

JACKMALIPAN/GETTY IMAGES ©

Mie Cafe This understated wooden house is home to some of best fusion flavours in town. (p57)

Sugar Palm Chef Kethana's Cambodian flavours are world-famous after cooking with Gordon Ramsay. (p59)

Best Cambodian Eats

Amok It does what it says on the sign, dishing up some of the best *amok* (baked fish) in town. (p62)

Bugs Cafe Experience Cambodian creepy crawlies in every shape and size at this alternative eatery. (p55)

Pot & Pan Restaurant Classic hole-in-the-wall cheapie that punches above its weight for presentation. (p53)

Road 60 Night Market Live like a local and dive into the street barbecues of this popular night market. (p53)

Best International Restaurants

Flow Go with the flow and experience creative flavours in a contemporary setting. (p60)

Le Malraux Experience a slice of Provence in the back alleys of the Old Market. (p59)

Mamma Shop Authentic Italian cooking just like Mamma made, if your mamma happens to be Italian. (p59)

Vibe Cafe Healthy vegan creations, probiotic super-

shakes and guilt-free desserts. (p60)

Best Good-Cause Restaurants

Bloom Cafe This training centre has creative cupcakes that are works of art. (p53)

Haven Immensely popular training restaurant with 'honest' food blending East and West. (p58)

Marum Operated by NGO Friends International, this delightful garden restaurant offers creative Khmer cuisine. (p53)

Spoons Cafe A well-regarded training restaurant run by EGBOK (Everything's Gonna Be OK). (p58)

Drinking & Nightlife

The transformation from sleepy overgrown village to an international destination for the jet set has been dramatic and Siem Reap is now firmly on the nightlife map of Southeast Asia. You don't have to fight for your right to party here; it's rockin' every night and the revelry goes on from dusk until dawn.

Pub St & Around

The heaving 'Pub St' area makes Siem Reap feel more like a beach town than a cultural capital. Pub St is closed to traffic every evening as food carts, drink carts and scores of party people take over. Great spots running parallel to Pub St include the Alley, to the south, plus a series of smaller lanes to the north. Late night, the crowd wanders on to Wat Preah Prohm Roth St and, eventually, to Sok San Rd, where there are a number of 'late-night' (read 'early morning') bars.

Beer Gardens

There are dozens of beer gardens around Siem Reap that are great places for a cheap beer and local snacks. All serve up ice-cold beer, some in 3L beer towers complete with chiller. The best strip is known locally as 'Cambodian Pub St'.

Hostel Bars & Happy Hours

Hostels bars are a big thing, drawing backpackers to guzzle shooters and play drinking games until the wee hours. Most bars have happy hours, as do some of the fancier hotels. Hitting the happy hours at some of the ritzier hotels is a good way to experience the high life on the cheap.

Best Cocktails

Asana Wooden House This unlikely countryside house in the city turns out some of the most authentic Cambodian cocktails in town. (p66)

Barcode Leading gay bar in town for classy cocktails and a nightly drag show. (p68)

MIKEINLONDON/GETTY IMAGES ©

Menaka Speakeasy Lounge
This 'secret' speakeasy
is hidden behind an Old
Market cafe and pays tribute
to the golden era of Cambodian rock 'n' roll. (p68)

Miss Wong Experience
the sassy Shanghai of the
1920s at this sophisticated
cocktail bar with designer
gins. (p66)

Picasso A convivial U-
shaped bar that has cheap
and cheerful cocktails during happy hour and all night
Wednesdays. (p67)

Best Late-Night Spots

Angkor What? The original
Pub St bar and still going
strong after two decades of
late-night drinking. (p68)

Laundry Bar Funky tunes,
leather couches and subtle
lighting, this is the place
for grown-ups seeking to
escape Pub St. (p67)

Soul Train Reggae Bar A
eulogy to Bob Marley and
friends, this bar is about
as chilled as it gets in Siem
Reap. (p67)

Temple Club Another long-
timer on Pub St, the volume
always seems to be turned
up to '11' here. (p70)

X Bar As the night wears
on, all-night drinkers are
drawn to the rooftop X like
moths to a lamp for breezes,
buckets and a skateboard
ramp. (p68)

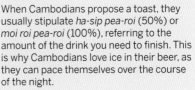

Top Tip

When Cambodians propose a toast, they
usually stipulate *ha-sip pea-roi* (50%) or
moi roi pea-roi (100%), referring to the
amount of the drink you need to finish. This
is why Cambodians love ice in their beer, as
they can pace themselves over the course
of the night.

Shopping

Despite the rough edges Siem Reap offers some smooth shopping opportunities. It is a hub for handicrafts produced by local artisans. There are also lots of good-cause shops where your purchasing power can make a difference to development. Kandal Village is an up-and-coming shopping destination with boutiques, galleries and cafes.

Local Products

Cambodia is famous for its exquisite silk, much of which is still traditionally hand-woven, and there are some famous silk weaving centres around Siem Reap. There are many skilled stone and wood carvers and silversmiths, and popular keepsakes include busts of Jayavarman VII and statues of Hindu deities.

Markets

When it comes to shopping in town, Psar Chaa is well stocked with anything you may want to buy in Cambodia, and lots you don't. Angkor Night Market is a popular place on the Siem Reap shopping scene and is well worth a browse to take advantage of cooler temperatures.

Shopping for a Cause

Several shops support Cambodia's disabled and disenfranchised through their production process or their profits. This is a worthy way to contribute to community development in Cambodia and shops sell everything including silk items, T-shirts, jewellery, handmade cards and more.

Temple Sellers

Don't forget to save some spending for the temples, as many of the villagers sell handicrafts, books and T-shirts and need a piece of the action. Some visitors get fed up with the endless sales pitches as they navigate the ancient wonders, while others enjoy the banter and a chance to interact with Cambodian people.

KONSTANTIN AKSENOV/SHUTTERSTOCK ©

Shopping for a Cause

AHA Fair Trade Village Extensive handicraft market supporting local producers from around Siem Reap Province. (p73)

Made in Cambodia Daily market at King's Road that promotes local artisans and their handmade wares. (p75)

Rajana Quirky boutique selling everything from original T-shirts to recycled jewellery. (p75)

Saomao Social enterprise with original jewellery made from bomb casings and old bullets. (p75)

Sra May Pick up a cotton *krama* (checked scarf) to protect from the elements at this social enterprise in Kandal Village. (p76)

Best Galleries

Eric Raisina Couture House Eric Raisina creates 'haute texture' fashion with his original creations. (p74)

McDermott Gallery Haunting images of Angkor produced in signature sepia from American photographer John McDermott. (p77)

Theam's House Original lacquerware creations and innovative art, set in one of the most beautiful gallery spaces in Cambodia. (p73)

Best for Silk

Angkor Silk Farm See the silk process from cocoon to creative clothing at this signature silk farm from Artisans Angkor. (p48)

IKTT A Japanese-run silk farm that creates beautiful traditional patterns using traditional methods. (p77)

Samatoa Experimenting with lotus, banana stem and more, Samatoa creates original soft silks with their own textures. (p73)

Soieries du Mekong Featuring handwoven silk creations; proceeds from sales help the remote Banteay Meanchey Province community. (p74)

Markets

Angkor Night Market The original night market and still the best despite many imitators, there is no need for air-con after dark. (p73)

Psar Chaa The Old Market is the commercial heart of downtown Siem Reap and offers a blend of local life and tourist kitsch. (p74)

Temple Views

So immense in size and scale is Angkor that it is one of the few ancient structures visible from space. Most people haven't got the US$20 million it takes to be a cosmonaut, so must go in search of their own atmosphere around Angkor. Whether you are seeking personal enlightenment or an inspired image, seek out some of these spectacular views.

Angkor Wat

Standing by the ponds watching a sunrise is superb, but it's equally rewarding to sit in the eastern gateway and watch the sun reveal the central tower. The views from the upper level are immense and help put the size and scale into perspective.

Angkor Thom

The gates of Angkor Thom almost floor you with their impact. The south gate is the most spectacular, but the east gate is the place for a serene view. Bayon is a jumble from afar, but during the early and late golden hours, the light can pick out the faces to bring it all to life.

Other Temples

Other views that should not be missed include the tree roots of Ta Prohm around opening time at 7.30am; approaching the mighty Preah Khan from the east in late afternoon; and seeing the pink sandstone of Banteay Srei begin to shimmer in the softer sunlight of late afternoon.

Sunrise & Sunset Spots

The most popular place for sunrise is Angkor Wat for obvious reasons. Sra Srang is usually pretty quiet, and can be spectacular thanks to reflections in the extensive waters. Phnom Bakheng and Pre Rup are also open for sunrise, but are more suited to sunset due to access issues in the dark.

Best for Sunrise or Sunset

Angkor Wat The definitive sunrise spot draws the crowds for a reason as dawn

VINCENT ST THOMAS/SHUTTERSTOCK ©

breaks behind this iconic temple. (p82)

Phnom Bakheng A hilltop temple overlooking Angkor Wat, this is the place for a bird's eye view of the Cambodian countryside. (p90)

Pre Rup This temple has beautiful views over the surrounding rice fields of the Eastern Baray. (p113)

Best for Jungle

Beng Mealea A jungle giant, this temple is almost the area of Angkor but has been swallowed by vines and creepers. (p130)

Kbal Spean This is the chance for a gentle jungle trek in the Angkor area. (p118)

Koh Ker A usurper capital from the 10th century, this extensive site is one of the most remote of all the Angkorian cities. (p126)

Ta Prohm The ultimate jungle temple: man overcomes nature to create, nature overcomes man to destroy. (p105)

Best for Film Buffs

Angkor Wat Used for the closing scenes of Wong Kar Wai's *In the Mood for Love*, it also featured in *Tomb Raider*. (p82)

Bayon When Lara Croft's Land Rover drops out of the sky in *Tomb Raider*, it lands near the Bayon and she burns off into the jungle. (p103)

Beng Mealea Part of Jean-Jacques Annaud's *Two*

Brothers was shot here as the family of tigers are seen in their temple home. (p130)

Ta Prohm This temple looks like it is straight out of a movie set and was a location for the original *Tomb Raider*. (p105)

Best of the Best

Banteay Samré Dating from the time of Angkor Wat, this temple has a unique inner moat and the remains of a rare sarcophagus. (p120)

Preah Neak Poan The ultimate water feature, Neak Poan is an elaborate series of decorative pools set on an island. (p113)

Ta Keo A 10th-century pyramid temple that looks more Mayan than Khmer; the stairs are steep but the views are worth it. (p107)

Massages & Spas

Reflecting Siem Reap's newfound status as an international destination, there are some super-swish spas and enough massage styles to rival the dining options. Try Chinese acupuncture, Japanese shiatsu, traditional Swedish, tough Thai or Vietnamese suction-cup massage. There are also massages by the blind and the infamous fish massages.

RUI DUANMU/EYEEM/GETTY IMAGES ©

Spas

Most of the leading luxury hotels and resorts have designer spas to indulge in a relaxing massage. Beyond the hotels, there are some stand-out spas that offer an array of rubs, scrubs and tubs.

Blind Massage

There are several outlets promoting massage by the blind to help create job opportunities for visually-impaired Cambodians. The surroundings are simple, but the massage is rewarding.

Foot or Fish Massage?

There are lots of cheap and cheerful massage shops around Psar Chaa and Pub St in Siem Reap. Some specialise in foot massage, while others offer a fish massage – aka a piranha pedicure – where lots of tiny cleaner fish nibble your dead skin.

Best Spas

Bodia Spa (☏063-761593; www.bodia-spa.com; Pithnou St; 1hr massage US$24-36; ☺10am-midnight) Bodia also offers its own range of herbal creations to help you unwind.

Frangipani Spa (☏063-964391; www.frangipani siemreap.com; 615 Hup Guan St; ☺10am-10pm) This was the business that kickstarted Kandal Village.

Lemongrass Garden (☏012 387385; www.lemon grassgarden.com; 105B Sivatha St; 1hr massage US$15-30; ☺11am-11pm) A popular spa on Sivatha St, innovations here include a family massage.

Best Massage by the Blind

Krousar Thmey (www.krousar-thmey.org; Charles de Gaulle Blvd; 1hr massage US$7; ☺9am-9pm) Set on the road to Angkor Wat.

Seeing Hands Massage 4 (☏012 836487; 324 Sivatha St; per fan/air-con US$5/7) The original blind massage innovator.

Cooking Courses

If you are really taken with Cambodian cuisine, it's possible to learn some tricks of the trade by signing up for a cooking course. This is a great way to introduce your Cambodian experience to your friends – no one wants to sit through the slide show of photos, but offer them a mouth-watering meal and they will all come running.

TOM COCKREM/GETTY IMAGES ©

Best Cooking Courses

Cooks in Tuk Tuks
(☏063-963400; www.cooksintuktuks.com; Siem Reap River Rd East; per person US$35) Cooks in Tuk Tuks is one of the original cooking classes in Siem Reap and still one of the best. Classes start at 10am daily with a visit to Psar Leu market, then return to their dedicated downtown school for a professional class.

Lily's Secret Garden Cooking Class (☏016 353621; www.lilysecretgarden.com; off Sombai Rd; per person US$24; ◷9am-1pm

& 3-7pm) This immersive cooking class takes place in a traditional Cambodian house on the outskirts of Siem Reap. Morning and afternoon sessions end in a three-course lunch or dinner. The price includes pick-up and drop-off in town.

Vegetarian Cooking Class (☏092 177127; http://peacecafeangkor.org; Siem Reap River Rd East; per person US$20) A vegetarian cooking class with tofu *amok*, papaya salad and vegie spring rolls on the menu.

Cambodian Cooking Cottage (☏077 566455; reservation@angkorw.com;

Wat Preah Prohm Roth St; per person US$25) This sophisticated cooking class in – surprise, surprise – a cottage near Wat Preah Prohm Roth includes tips on decorative presentation, a recipe book, a DVD and some takeaway spices.

Le Tigre de Papier (☏012 265811; www.angkor-cooking-class-cambodia.com; Pub St; per person US$15) Classes include a visit to the market and the chance to prepare an *amok* degustation, a variation on the national dish. Daily classes are held at 10am, 1pm and 5pm.

Four Perfect Days

Day 1

CAO WEI/GETTY IMAGES ©

Beat the crowds with an early morning countryside jaunt to **Banteay Srei** (pictured; p117), the art gallery of Angkor. Continue out to **Kbal Spean** (p118), but before starting the jungle trek, drop into the **Angkor Centre for Conservation of Biodiversity** (p119) and join their 9am wildlife tour.

Enjoy a local lunch at **Borey Sovann Restaurant** (p119), then stop to visit the inspirational and educational **Cambodia Landmine Museum** (p120) and the nearby **Banteay Srei Butterfly Centre** (p120).

Sample some Cambodian flavours at **Amok** (p62) or **Khmer Kitchen Restaurant** (p54). If you have the stamina, explore some of the alleys and lanes surrounding Pub St for a nightcap.

Day 2

LEISA TYLER/ALAMY STOCK PHOTO ©

Set out early and make for the north gate of **Ta Prohm** (p105) around 7am to beat the crowds. Look at the jungle canopy from a different angle at the **Angkor Zipline** (p33), an adrenaline ride through the treetops.

Try a local lunch at one of the **Sra Srang** (p107) eateries and then head for **Angkor Thom** (p92). Tackle the **Angkor Thom Walk** that takes in the best of the temples.

Celebrate the scale of the sights today with a stylish contemporary meal at **Cuisine Wat Damnak** (pictured; p66) or **Mie Cafe** (p57). If you already have your glad rags on, then continue to classy cocktail bar **Miss Wong** (p66).

Day 3

SL-PHOTOGRAPHY/SHUTTERSTOCK ©

Hit the Tonlé Sap lake and the stilted village of **Kompong Khleang** (pictured; p140), one of the largest villages on the great lake. Explore by boat and visit some of the floating houses on the water.

Continue to the vast jungle temple of **Beng Mealea** (p130), located about 70km from Siem Reap. Book an early lunch at **Sreymom Beng Mealea Homestay** (p131) and then explore the temple from the remote eastern end.

The rest of the afternoon is free to enjoy **Siem Reap** (p29). Browse the shops of **Kandal Village** (p38) and the local **markets** (p36, book a **massage or spa treatment** (p18). In the evening, experience a dazzling performance by **Phare the Cambodian Circus** (p71).

Day 4

BATTERER MEDIA/SHUTTERSTOCK ©

Patience is a virtue and it's time to be rewarded with the mother of all sunrises at **Angkor Wat** (p82). Set out in the pitch black and make for the back door on the east side, avoiding the crowds flooding in on the western causeway. Stick around when the tour groups trot back to town before breakfast and explore while it is relatively quiet.

In the afternoon, sign up for a Cambodian **cooking class** (p19) to take some culinary secrets home. If you want to continue the culinary theme into the night, try an after-dark tour by **Vespa** (p33), or celebrate the last night in town with a DIY pub crawl in the Old Market area, including legendary local spots such as **Asana Wooden House** (p66) and **Laundry Bar** (p67).

Need to Know

For detailed information, see Survival Guide p143

Languages
Khmer, English,
Chinese, French

Currency
riel (r); US dollars (US$)
universally accepted

Visas
A one-month tourist
visa costs US$30 on
arrival and requires one
passport-sized photo.
Easily extendable
business visas are
available for US$35.

Money
ATMs are widely
available. Credit cards
are accepted by many
hotels and restaurants.

Mobile Phones
Roaming is possible
but it is expensive.
Local SIM cards and
unlocked mobile
phones are readily
available.

Area Code
Cambodia: 855
Siem Reap: 063

Time
Indochina Time (UTC/
GMT plus seven hours)

Daily Budget

Budget: Less than US$50
Dorm or cheap guesthouse room: US$5–15
Cafe and street eats: US$1–5
Short *moto* trip: US$0.50–1

Midrange: US$50–200
Smart hotel room: US$20–50
Midrange local restaurant meal: US$5–15
Guided tour: from US$25

Top end: More than US$200
Boutique hotel or resort: US$80–500
Gastronomic meal with drinks: US$25–50
Car rental per day: from US$30

Advance Planning

○ Make sure your passport is valid for at least six months
beyond the date of arrival.

○ Arrange any recommended inoculations at a travel-health
clinic.

○ Arrange for appropriate travel insurance.

○ Check the airline baggage restrictions.

○ Inform your debit-/credit-card company you're heading
away.

○ Check to make sure you can obtain a visa-on-arrival in
Cambodia.

Arriving in Siem Reap

Siem Reap is the transport hub for this region. There is an international airport, as well as international bus services to Thailand.

✈ By Air

Flights arrive at Siem Reap International Airport (p145), 7km west of the town centre.

Taxis Official taxis are available next to the terminal for US$9. A trip to the city centre on the back of a *moto* is US$3 or US$7 by *remork-moto*.

🚢 By Boat

There are daily express boat services between Siem Reap and Phnom Penh or Battambang.

🚌 By Bus

Buses connect Siem Reap with major destinations around the country, including Phnom Penh, Battambang and Preah Vihear City (Tbeng Meanchey).

Getting Around

Siem Reap is a breeze to get around, whether under your own steam or by hiring a driver.

🚲 Bike

Some guesthouses around town hire out bicycles, as do a few shops around Psar Chaa.

🚗 Car & Motorcycle

Most hotels and guesthouses can organise car hire for the day. Motorcycle hire is widely available.

🏍 Moto

A *moto* (unmarked motorcycle taxi) with a driver will cost from US$10 per day. Far-flung temples involve a higher fee.

🛺 Remork-Moto

Remork-motos (*tuk tuks*), and are a nice way to get around. Local fares are about US$2 to US$5, while touring the temples starts from US$15 per day.

Siem Reap & Angkor Neighbourhoods

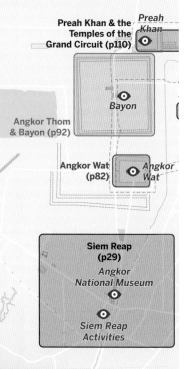

**Ta Prohm & the Temples
of the Small Circuit (p104)**

⊙ *Ta Prohm*

Temples of Angkor (p79)
A source of inspiration and national
pride to Khmers, the temples of
Angkor are unrivalled in scale
and grandeur in Southeast Asia.
Most famous among these is
Angkor Wat, the heart and soul of
Cambodia and the world's largest
religious site. Nearby, Preah Khan,
Ta Prohm, the Ruluos temples and
monumental Angkor Thom are just
as impressive.

Further afield, don't miss
Banteay Srei, Koh Ker, Beng Mealea
and Tonlé Sap.

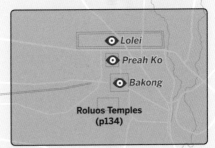

⊙ *Lolei*

⊙ *Preah Ko*

⊙ *Bakong*

**Roluos Temples
(p134)**

Explore

Siem Reap

Temples of Angkor

Performer at Angkor Wat (p82) GAVIN GOUGH/GETTY IMAGES ©

Siem Reap

Siem Reap (see -em ree- ep; សៀមរាប) has emerged as the epicentre of chic Cambodia, with everything from backpacker party pads to hip hotels, world-class wining and dining across a range of cuisines, sumptuous spas, great shopping, local tours to suit both foodies and adventurers, and a creative cultural scene that includes Cambodia's leading contemporary circus.

Siem Reap is still a small town at heart and is easy enough to navigate on foot, by bicycle or with local transport. The historic centre is around Psar Chaa (Old Market) and nearby Pub St, and this is the epicentre of life in the city, including cafes, restaurants, bars and shops.

Most people are in Siem Reap for the temples of Angkor, but there are plenty of things to keep visitors busy in and around Siem Reap, including some impressive museums covering everything from the temples to textiles, handicraft centres and a large number of colourful pagodas.

Siem Reap is also an emerging activity centre with cooking classes, foodie experiences, spa journeys, cycling tours, motorbike adventures, birdwatching trips and a whole lot more.

Getting There & Around

Siem Reap International Airport is a major gateway to northwest Cambodia and offers connections to regional cities. There are international buses to Bangkok, as well as buses to major Cambodian cities. There are also express boat services to Phnom Penh and Battambang.

Neighbourhood Maps on p42, p44 and p46

Night market COCOS.BOUNTY/SHUTTERSTOCK ©

Top Sight

Angkor National Museum

Looming large on the road to Angkor is the Angkor National Museum, a state-of-the-art showpiece on the Khmer civilisation and the majesty of Angkor. It offers a very insightful experience for first-time visitors, putting the historically complex story of Angkor and the Khmer empire in context before exploring the temples. While the National Museum in Phnom Penh boasts a bigger collection, the presentation of the artefacts here is cutting edge.

⊙ MAP P44, D1

សារមន្ទីរជាតិអង្គរ

www.angkornational
museum.com

968 Charles de Gaulle Blvd

adult/child under 1.2m
US$12/6

⊗ 8.30am-6pm May-Sep,
to 6.30pm Oct-Apr

Museum Highlights

Displays are themed by era, religion and royalty as visitors move through the impressive galleries. After a short introductory presentation, visitors enter the Zen-like Gallery of a Thousand Buddhas, which has a fine collection of images. Other exhibits include the pre-Angkorian periods of Funan and Chenla; the great Khmer kings; Angkor Wat; and Angkor Thom.

Some of the standout pieces in the collection include a late 12th-/early 13th-century seated Buddha sheltered by a *naga* (mythical serpent-being); a 7th-century standing Vishnu from Sambor Prei Kuk in Kompong Thom; and a stunning 10th-century lintel from the beautiful temple of Banteay Srei.

Exhibits include touchscreen video, epic commentary and the chance to experience a panoramic sunrise at Angkor Wat. The audio tour is useful for those who want a more comprehensive understanding of the exhibits on display.

Nearby: Angkor Conservation

Angkor Conservation (Siem Reap River Rd West; US$5; ⏲ unofficially 8am-5pm) is a Ministry of Culture compound that houses more than 5000 statues, *lingas* (phallic symbols) and inscribed stelae, stored here to protect them from the wanton looting that has blighted hundreds of sites around Angkor. The finest statuary is hidden away inside Angkor Conservation's warehouses, meticulously numbered and catalogued. While it's not officially open to the public, it's sometimes possible to get a peek at the collection for a fee. It's located just a short walk north along the river from the museum.

★ **Top Tips**

o As the museum is entirely air-conditioned, plan a visit during the middle of the day to avoid the sweltering midday temperatures at the temples.

o Audio tours are available in Chinese, English, French, German, Japanese, Korean, Russian, Spanish and Thai for US$5.

o Wheelchairs are available free of charge for visitors with mobility impairment.

o Allow about two hours to visit the museum in depth and to stop by the shop and small cafe at the end of your visit.

✕ **Take a Break**

Across the road from the museum, Pho Yong (p56) specialises in Vietnam's national dish. On the nearby east bank of the Siem Reap River, enjoy eclectic Khmer flavours at Marum (p53).

Top Experience

Siem Reap Activities

It may be the temples of Angkor that draw visitors to Cambodia in the millions, but Siem Reap is no slouch when it comes to entertaining the masses. There are a host of activities on offer including two-wheeled tours on bicycles and motorbikes deep into the Cambodian countryside, as well as gentle quad-bike adventures through surrounding villages. For a bigger adrenaline rush, zipline through the jungle canopy.

All the activity operators mentioned here have a base in Siem Reap, but most will offer guesthouse or hotel pick-up, or arrange to meet at a central location.

Cycling Tours

Pedal-powered adventures include village tours, temple back roads and challenging rides to more remote sites. **KKO** (Khmer for Khmer Organisation; Map p46, A1; ☑093 903024; www.kko-cambodia.org; Taphul Rd; tours US$35-60) offers great tours around the paths of Angkor and beyond the Western Baray. To experience local life, including lunch with a local family, take a half-day tour with **PURE!** (Map p46, F2; ☑097 2356862; Hup Guan St; per person US$25-35) around Siem Reap. For rides through the countryside or a temple tour on two wheels, try **Grasshopper Adventures** (Map p46, H5; ☑012 462165; www.grasshopperadventures.com; 586 St 26; per person from US$39; ☺7am-8pm).

Motorbike Tours

Some great dirt-bike tours go deep into remote Cambodia, but these require serious experience. For something more gentle, try riding pillion on a Vespa, a cut above the average *moto*. **Cambodia Vespa Adventures** (Map p42, E1; ☑012 861610; www.vespaadventures-sr.com; P64 Borey Prem Prey; tours per person US$75-126) and **Vespa Adventures** (☑017 881384; http://vespaadventures.com/siem-reap-bike-tours; tours US$70-115) both offer a great way to check out street-food offerings after dark in the company of knowledgeable local guides.

Quad Biking

Quad bikes or ATVs are a stable way to explore the countryside around Siem Reap at a leisurely pace. **Quad Adventure Cambodia** (Map p44, C8; ☑092 787216; www.quad-adventure-cambodia.com; Country Rd Laurent; sunset ride US$30, full day US$170) and **Cambodia Quad Bike** (Map p44, D8; ☑012 893447; www.cambodiaquadbike.com; Sala Kamreuk Rd; 1hr/half day US$30/100) offer rice fields at sunset and back roads through traditional villages.

★ **Top Tips**

o Take a sunset quad-bike ride for beautiful views over the surrounding rice fields.

o Combine Angkor Zipline with a visit to the jungle temples of Ta Nei and Ta Prohm, just a short distance away.

o For those who prefer to go their own way, it's possible to cycle around the walls of Angkor Thom for views of the moat and jungle.

★ **Ziplining**

Angkor provides the ultimate backdrop for this zipline experience, although you won't actually see the temples while navigating the course. **Angkor Zipline** (off Map p42, F1; ☑096 999 9100; www.angkorzipline.com; short/full course US$60/100; ☺6am-5pm) is located inside the Angkor protected area. The course includes 10 ziplines, 21 treetop platforms, four skybridges, a tandem line and an abseil finish, plus a panoramic rest stop.

Walking Tour 🚶

Siem Reap Stroll

Explore the contemporary, colonial and spiritual side of Siem Reap with this riverside walk that takes in the best of Temple Town. Head out in the later afternoon to take advantage of cooling temperatures and to see the Preah Ang Chek Preah Ang Chorm shrine busy with locals. Finish up with a happy hour cocktail at one of the leading colonial-era hotels.

Walk Facts

Start Psar Chaa

End Raffles Grand Hotel d'Angkor

Length 4km; two to three hours, depending on stops

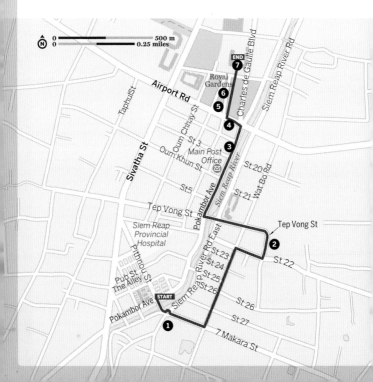

❶ Wat Dam Nak

Start off at the bustling centre of commerce that is Psar Chaa (p74). Cross the river and make for **Wat Dam Nak** (p51), formerly a royal palace and now an active temple which houses the Centre for Khmer Studies and its library.

❷ Wat Bo

Wind your way east to Wat Bo Rd, a lively strip of cafes, restaurants and bars, and head to the eponymous wat. **Wat Bo** (p48) is one of the oldest temples in Siem Reap and has a beautiful sweeping roof and some of the best-preserved old frescoes seen in town. If you are here sometime after 4pm, you may hear the resident monks chanting.

❸ FCC Angkor

Leave Wat Bo Rd and head west across the Siem Reap River, passing the Main Post Office. Wander north up the river and you will pass the **FCC Angkor** (p60), a striking piece of architecture that was once an official residence of the French Governor General in Cambodia.

❹ Royal Residence

Continuing north, King Sihamoni's **royal residence** (Airport Rd), dating from the 1950s, is located near the river, although it looks a rather humble dwelling now

that it is overshadowed by all the luxury resorts and boutique hotels around town.

❺ Preah Ang Chek Preah Ang Chorm

Just west of the royal residence, the shrine of **Preah Ang Chek Preah Ang Chorm** (p49) is said to represent two Angkorian princesses. The much revered statues draw locals praying for luck.

❻ Royal Gardens

Next to the shrine are the tall trees of the **Royal Gardens**, home to a resident colony of fruit bats that take off to feed on insects around dusk.

❼ Raffles Grand Hotel d'Angkor

Finish with a well-earned cocktail at the comfortable Elephant Bar at **Raffles Grand Hotel d'Angkor** (☏063-963888; www.raffles.com; 1 Charles de Gaulle Blvd; r incl breakfast from US$220; ❄@☎☼). Happy hour is from 5pm to 9pm.

✗ Take a Break

Just off Wat Bo Rd, **Pages Cafe** (p56) turns out tapas and is also good for a caffeine fix. Linger at atmospheric **FCC Angkor** (p60) for a drink or a meal from their Asian-flavoured menu.

Walking Tour 🥾

Psar Chaa (Old Market)

Psar Chaa (Old Market), the commercial heart of old Siem Reap, is a traditional market that attracts local shoppers and international browsers in equal numbers. The market is a game of two halves – one filled with fresh produce, exotic fruits and homewares; the other with handicrafts, fake antiques, textiles and clothing.

Walk Facts

Start Scales of Justice

End Siem Reap Art Center

Length 420m; one hour, depending on stops

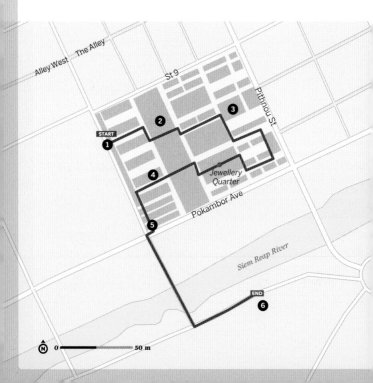

❶ The Scales of Justice

Start on the northwestern side of the market at the **Scales of Justice**, a pair of weighing scales placed here to settle any disputes between vendor and customer over the precise weight of an item. If you smell something fishy about this, that would be the stalls of dried fish nearby, an essential way to preserve the daily catch.

❷ Feeling Fruity

Head east deeper into the market and you will discover the fresh produce section, where colourful heaps of fruit and vegetables, familiar and foreign, are piled high. You may want to buy something as a pick-me-up for when exploring the temples.

❸ Accessories & Souvenirs

Emerging on the other side of the food area, you will come across cheap accessories such as shoes and backpacks – some fake, some the real deal. Explore the aisles of trinkets, souvenirs and statues, keeping in mind much of it may be imported from neighbouring countries.

❹ The Perfect T-Shirt

Pass through the jewellery quarter of the market, a separate shop within the market, before emerging on the other side in a clothing section where lots of seconds from the garment factories turn up. Tin Tin au Cambodge, Danger Mines! and Angkor Wat T-shirts are also widely available.

❺ Good-Cause Shopping

Swerve left at the western side of the market passing recycled bags and some creative *krama* (checked scarf) clothing and head to the southern side where there is the good-cause store **Susu** (www.susu cambodia.com; Psar Chaa; ☎1-10pm Mon-Fri, 2-10pm Sat & Sun). Handicrafts are sold to help women's development in Cambodia.

❻ Siem Reap Art Center

Finally, head across the river on a traditional wooden bridge to the **Siem Reap Art Center** (p77) for more handicrafts and souvenirs. Or call it a day at the market, around where you won't look long for a cafe or bar.

Walking Tour 🥾

Kandal Village Stroll

Kandal Village is the name for an emerging shopping strip located on Hup Guan St, which is chock-full of galleries and cafes. It is a top place to wander during the heat of the day, when temperatures at the temples may be debilitating, or during a rainy season downpour. Plan to stop for lunch at one of the great little eateries here along the way.

Walk Facts

Start Bloom Cafe

End Common Grounds

Length 320m; one to three hours, depending on stops

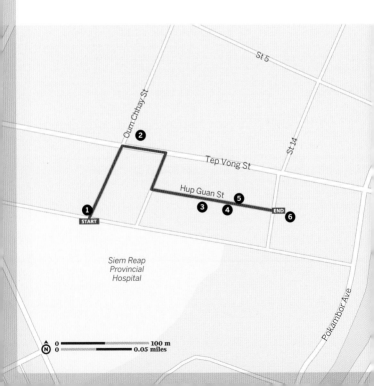

❶ A Blooming Business

Start off in **Bloom Cafe** (p53), a good-cause enterprise that turns food into art with some of the most delightful cupcakes in Cambodia. The sugar rush should sustain you until later.

❷ Child Support

Veer briefly away from Hup Guan St to visit the **Angkor Hospital for Children Visitor's Centre** (AHC; ☎ 063-963409; www.angkor hospital.org; cnr Oum Chhay & Tep Vong Sts; ⏰24hr), which informs visitors about their important work to support pediatrics in Siem Reap and also has some handicrafts for sale.

❸ Shopping for a Cause

Soieries du Mekong (p74) is a silk emporium that produces exquisite scarves in the remote village of Banteay Chhmar to support vulnerable women and create employment in rural areas. Close by, and on the same side of the street, is **Sra May** (p76), a social enterprise offering traditional products such as palm-leaf boxes and handwoven *krama*.

❹ Quirky Fashion

There are some very fashionable places on this strip and **trunkh.** (p73) is one of them. You'll find unusual items, stylish clothing, home furnishings, art and more here.

❺ Temple Wear

Established by French-Cambodian fashion designer Sirivan Chak Dumas, **Sirivan** (p76) offers an elegant collection of women's and men's clothing made in light linen and cotton, perfect for exploring the temples in high humidity.

❻ Coffee Time

Wind down with a drink at **Common Grounds** (p56), a modern coffee shop assisting Cambodians with English and computing classes. Just a few doors down, **Vibe Cafe** (p60) is a vegan cafe offering 'cleansing juices' made with exotic ingredients.

Walking Tour 🥾

Pub St Pub Crawl

Pub St and the Angkor What? bar have become almost as renowned as the temples of Angkor to generations of backpackers. While Pub St draws the headlines and the revellers, there is a whole series of lanes and alleys criss-crossing the old French quarter in this part of town that make a great location to embark on a bar crawl.

Walk Facts

Start Asana Wooden House

End X Bar

Length 600m; three to four hours, depending on stops

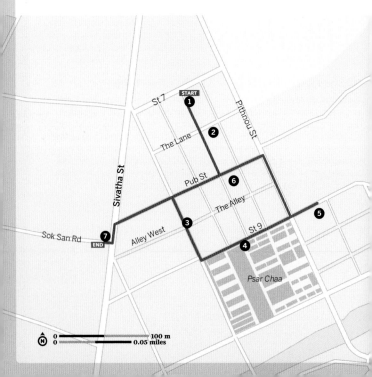

❶ The Wooden House

Kick off your night with an early evening cocktail at **Asana Wooden House** (p66), an impressive country residence in the backstreets of Siem Reap. Infused rice wine is used to give creative cocktails a kick.

❷ Shanghai Style

Miss Wong (p66), an old Shanghai-themed cocktail bar with a touch of class, serves Death's Door Gin and apricot and kaffir lime martinis. Expect a well-heeled expat crowd.

❸ Beatnik Bar

It's time to traverse Pub St and head into the Alley. Stop at the atmospheric corner bar that is **Beatnik Bar** (p68) and discover that hipsters existed back in the 1950s, only without the beards.

❹ Old Market

Stop for a local dinner at one of the many Cambodian food stalls on the northwestern side of **Psar Chaa** (Old Market; p54). The Khmer eats here are either pre-made or cooked fresh.

❺ Dirty Laundry

Just around the corner, **Laundry Bar** (p67) is a Siem Reap institution. It's popular with the Francophone crowd in town for its mellow vibe and central pool table.

❻ Angkor What?

It's time to head to Pub St where the volume is permanently cranked up to 11. Start with the one and only **Angkor What?** (p68), which claims to have been promoting irresponsible drinking since 1998.

❼ X Marks the Spot

Finish with a nightcap at **X Bar** (p68), at the western end of Pub St. It's one of the late-night spots in town. Keep yourself entertained with pool, table football or the skateboard pipe (though drink-skateboarding may not be wise!) until the sun comes up.

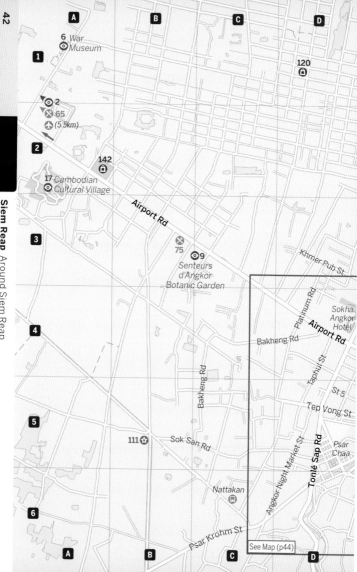

Siem Reap Around Siem Reap

A

B

C

D

1

6 War Museum

120

2

65

(5.5km)

142

17 Cambodian Cultural Village

Airport Rd

3

75

9

Senteurs d'Angkor Botanic Garden

Khmer Pub St

Platinum Rd

Sokha Angkor Hotel

Airport Rd

Bakheng Rd

Taphul St

St 5

4

Bakheng Rd

Tep Vong St

5

111

Sok San Rd

Angkor Night Market St

Tonlé Sap Rd

Psar Chaa

6

Nattakan

Psar Krohm St

See Map (p44)

A

B

C

D

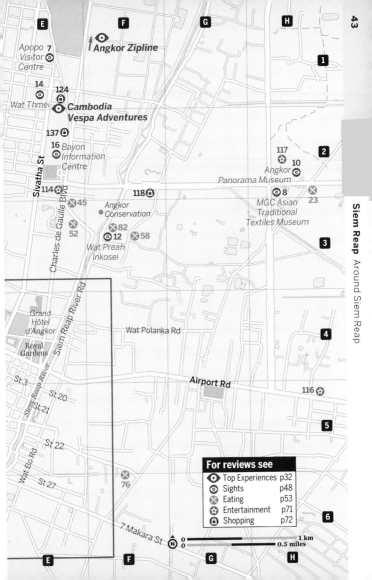

E

Apopo **7**
Visitor
Centre

14
Wat Thmei

124
Cambodia
Vespa Adventures

137

16 Bayon
Information
Centre

Sivatha St

114

Charles de Gaulle Blvd

45

52

Angkor
Conservation

82

12 **58**

Wat Preah
Inkosei

F
Angkor Zipline

118

G

H

1

117 **10**

2

Angkor
Panorama Museum

8

23

MGC Asian
Traditional
Textiles Museum

3

Grand
Hôtel
d'Angkor

Royal
Gardens

Siem Reap River Rd

Siem Reap River

St 3

St 20
St 21

St 22

Wat Bo Rd

St 27

76

Wat Polanka Rd

Airport Rd

116

4

5

7 Makara St

For reviews see
◉ Top Experiences p32
◉ Sights   p48
✪ Eating   p53
✪ Entertainment p71
🔒 Shopping   p72

0 ————— 1 km
0 ————— 0.5 miles

6

E   **F**   **G**   **H**

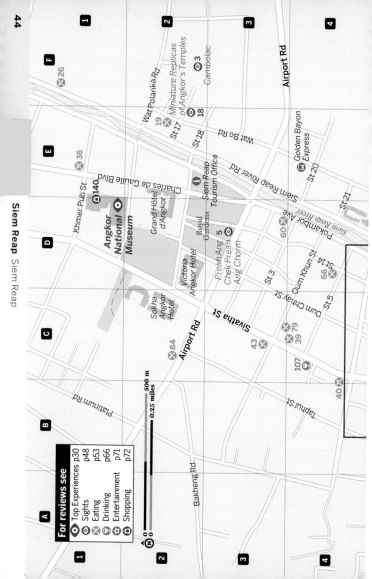

44

Siem Reap Siem Reap

For reviews see
- ◎ Top Experiences p30
- ◎ Sights p48
- ⊗ Eating p53
- ◍ Drinking p66
- ⊕ Entertainment p71
- ⬢ Shopping p72

500 m
0.25 miles

Angkor National Museum

Sokha Angkor Hotel

Grand Hôtel d'Angkor

Victoria Angkor Hotel

Royal Gardens

Siem Reap Tourism Office

Miniature Replicas of Angkor's Temples

Cambolac

Wat Polanka Rd

Charles de Gaulle Blvd

Khmer Pub St

Platinum Rd

Airport Rd

Bakheng Rd

Sivatha St

Taphul St

Oum Chhay St

Oum Khun St

Pokambor Ave

Siem Reap River

Siem Reap River Rd

Wat Bo Rd

St 17

St 18

St 20

St 21

St 3

St 5

St 14

Golden Bayon Express

Preah Ang Chek Preah Ang Chorm

26

36

84

140

19

18

3

5

60

43

79

39

107

40

66

Siem Reap Siem Reap

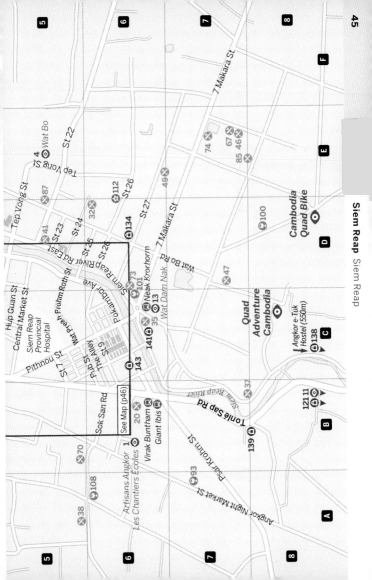

Wat Bo

Tep Vong St

St 22

St 26

St 27

7 Makara St

7 Makara St

Tep Vong St

Hup Guan St

Central Market St

Siem Reap Provincial Hospital

Pithnou St

St 17

St 23

St 24

St 25

St 26

Wat Bo Rd

Wat Dam Nak

St 9

Pub St

The Alley

Wat Preah Prohm Roth St

Pokambor Ave

Siem Reap River Rd East

Sok San Rd

Psar Krohm St

Angkor Night Market St

Tonlé Sap Rd

Tonlé Sap Rd

Siem Reap River

Cambodia Quad Bike

Quad Adventure Cambodia

Angkor e-Tuk Hostel (550m)

Les Chantiers Écoles

Artisans Angkor

Virak Buntham

Giant Ibis

Neak Krorhorm

See Map (p46)

4

87

41

112

32

134

49

74

67

46

85

100

47

37

143

141

35

13

101

3

20

1

108

38

70

139

121 11

138

93

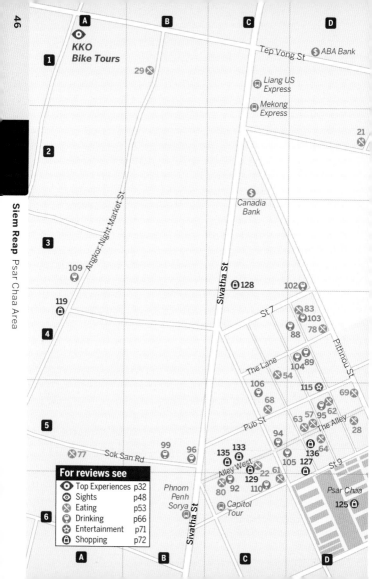

KKO
Bike Tours

29 ⊗

Tep Vong St   ⑤ ABA Bank

⑪ Liang US
Express

⑪ Mekong
Express

21 ⊗

⑤
Canadia
Bank

Angkor Night Market St

Sivatha St

⑪ 128   102 ⑫

109 ⑫

119 ⑪

St 7

⊗ 83
⑫ 103
88 ⑫   78

The Lane   ⑫ 89
⊗ 54   104

106   115 ☆
68 ⑫   69 ⊗

Pub St   ⑫ 63 57 95 62 ⊗
94   136 ⊗ 64   The Alley
⑪   28
135 133   105 127
80 ⊗ 92   ⑪
99 ⑫   96 ⑫   Alley West   St 9
⊗ 77   Sok San Rd   22 61
129 110

Pithnou St

Phnom
Penh
Sorya   ⑪ Capitol
Tour   Psar Chaa

125 ⑪

Sivatha St

For reviews see

⊙	Top Experiences	p32
⊙	Sights	p48
⊗	Eating	p53
⑫	Drinking	p66
☆	Entertainment	p71
⑪	Shopping	p72

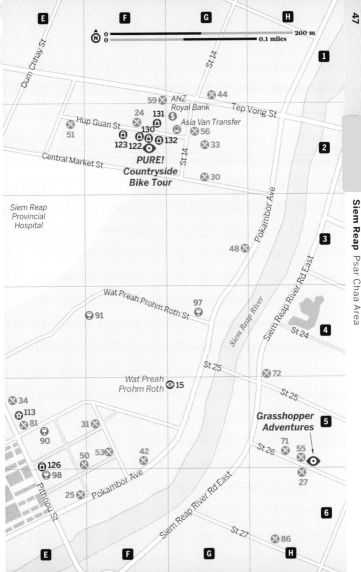

Sights

Artisans Angkor – Les Chantiers Écoles

ARTS CENTRE

1 ⊙ MAP P44, B6

Siem Reap is the epicentre of the drive to revitalise Cambodian traditional culture, which was dealt a harsh blow by the Khmer Rouge and the years of instability that followed its rule. Les Chantiers Écoles teaches wood- and stone-carving techniques, traditional silk painting, lacquerware and other artisan skills to impoverished young Cambodians. Free guided tours explaining traditional techniques are available daily from 7.30am to 6.30pm. Tucked down a side road, the school is well signposted from Sivatha St.

On the premises the school runs a beautiful shop called Artisans Angkor (p72), which sells everything from sculptures to homewares. All profits fund the school.Les Chantiers Écoles also maintains and offers free tours of a silk farm. (សិប្បករអង្គរ; www.artisansdangkor. com; admission free; ⊙7.30am-6.30pm)

Angkor Silk Farm

FARM

2 ⊙ MAP P42, A1

Les Chantiers Écoles (p48) maintains the Angkor Silk Farm, which produces some of the best work in the country, including clothing, interior-design products and accessories. All stages of the production process can be seen here, from the cultivation of mulberry trees to the nurturing of silkworms to the dyeing and weaving of silk. Free tours are available daily. A free shuttle bus departs from Les Chantiers Écoles in Siem Reap at 9.30am and 1.30pm.

The farm is about 16km west of Siem Reap, just off the road to Sisophon in the village of Puok. (www.artisansdangkor.com; admission free; ⊙7.30am-5.30pm)

Cambolac

ARTS CENTRE

3 ⊙ MAP P44, F2

Cambodia has a long tradition of producing beautiful lacquerware, although the years of upheaval resulted in some of the skills being lost. Cambolac is a social enterprise helping to restore Cambodia's lacquer tradition and create a new contemporary scene. You can tour the workshop to learn more about the perfectionist approach required to produce a piece. Most of the guides are hearing-impaired and a tour allows some great interaction and the opportunity to learn some basic sign language.

It's a worthy cause with some beautiful handmade souvenirs for sale. (ខេមបូឡាក់; ☎088 355 6078; http://cambolac.com; Wat Polanka; admission free; ⊙8-11.30am & 1-5pm Mon-Sat)

Wat Bo

BUDDHIST TEMPLE

4 ⊙ MAP P44, E5

This is one of the town's oldest temples and has a collection of well-preserved wall paintings from the late 19th century depicting the *Reamker,* Cambodia's interpretation of the *Ramayana*. The monks here regularly chant sometime between 4.30pm and 6pm and this can be a spellbinding and spiritual moment if you happen to be visiting. (តេប; Tep Vong St; admission free; ⊘6am-6pm)

Preah Ang Chek Preah Ang Chorm BUDDHIST SHRINE

5 ◉ MAP P44, D3

Located just west of the royal residence is the shrine of Preah Ang Chek Preah Ang Chorm. Said to represent two Angkorian princesses, these sacred statues were originally housed at the Preah Poan gallery in Angkor Wat, but were moved all over Siem Reap for their protection from invaders, eventually settling here in 1990. Locals throng here to pray for luck, especially newlyweds, and it is an atmospheric place to visit around dusk, as the incense smoke swirls around.

Next to the shrine are the tall trees of the Royal Gardens, home to a resident colony of fruit bats (also known as flying foxes) that take off to feed on insects around dusk. (ព្រះអង្គចេក ព្រះអង្គចម; Royal Gardens; admission free; ⊘6am-10pm)

War Museum MUSEUM

6 ◉ MAP P42, A1

The unique selling point here is that the museum encourages visitors to handle the old weapons, from an AK-47 right through to a rocket launcher. We're not sure what health and safety think about it, but it makes for a good photo

Silkworm cocoons

op. Other war junk includes Soviet-era T-54 tanks and MiG-19 fighters. Former soldiers act as tour guides. (សារមន្ទីរប្រវត្តិសាស្ត្រសង្គ្រាម; ☏097 457 8666; www.warmuseum cambodia.com; Kaksekam Village; admission incl guide US$5; ⊘7am-5pm)

Apopo Visitor Centre
VISITOR CENTRE

7 ◉ MAP P42, E1

Meet the hero rats that are helping to clear landmines in Cambodia. Apopo has trained the highly sensitive, almost-blind Gambian pouched rat to sniff explosives, which dramatically speeds up the detection of mines in the countryside. The visitor centre gives background on the work of Apopo, with a short video and the chance to meet the rats themselves. (☏081 599237; www.apopo.org; Koumai Rd; US$5; ⊘8.30am-5.30pm Mon-Sat)

MGC Asian Traditional Textiles Museum
MUSEUM

8 ◉ MAP P42, H2

This museum showcases the best in Asian textiles from around the Mekong region, including Cambodia, Laos, Myanmar and Thailand, as well as from India. There is a variety of galleries showing the weaving process in each country and a mix of traditional and contemporary galleries showing different regional costumes past and present. (សារមន្ទីរវាយនភណ្ឌប្រពៃណីអាស៊ី អ៊ីម ជី ស៊ី; www.mgcattmuseum.com; Rd 60; adult/child under 12 US$3/free; ⊘8.30am-4pm, closed Tue)

Soviet-era tanks, War Museum (p49)

HEINZTEH/SHUTTERSTOCK ©

Senteurs d'Angkor Botanic Garden
GARDENS

9 ◉ MAP P42, C3

The botanic garden of Senteurs d'Angkor (p75) is a sort of Willy Wonka's for the senses, where you can sample infused teas and speciality coffees in the on-site cafe. More a laboratory than a garden, they also make soaps, oils and perfumes here. (Airport Rd; ⏱7.30am-5.30pm)

Angkor Panorama Museum
MUSEUM

10 ◉ MAP P42, H2

Donated by the North Korean government, this stylish building conceals an incredible panoramic painting that is 13m high and 123m around. The detail is stunning, with many of the figures such as the Buddhist monks extremely lifelike. Apparently it took almost three years to complete, but this still doesn't really justify the entry fee. (សារមន្ទីរសួគទស្សនៈអង្គរ; ☎063-766215; http://angkorpanoramamuseum.com; Rd 60; US$15; ⏱9am-8pm)

Wat Athvea
BUDDHIST TEMPLE

11 ◉ MAP P44, B8

South of the city centre, Wat Athvea is an attractive pagoda on the site of an ancient temple. The old temple is still in very good condition and sees far fewer visitors than the main temples in the Angkor area, making it a peaceful spot in the late afternoon. (វត្តអថ្វា;

incl in Angkor admission 1/3/7 days US$37/62/72; ⏱6am-6pm)

Wat Preah Inkosei
BUDDHIST TEMPLE

12 ◉ MAP P42, F3

This wat north of town is built on the site of an early Angkorian brick temple, which still stands today at the rear of the compound. (វត្តព្រះឥន្ទកោសិយ៍; admission free; ⏱6am-6pm)

Wat Dam Nak
BUDDHIST TEMPLE

13 ◉ MAP P44, C6

Formerly a royal palace during the reign of King Sisowath, hence the name *dam nak* (palace), today Wat Dam Nak is home to the Center for Khmer Studies (www.khmerstudies.org), an independent institution promoting a greater understanding of Khmer culture with a drop-in research library on-site. (វត្តដំណាក់; admission free; ⏱6am-6pm)

Wat Thmei
BUDDHIST TEMPLE

14 ◉ MAP P42, E1

Wat Thmei has a small memorial stupa containing the skulls and bones of victims of the Khmer Rouge. It also has plenty of young monks eager to practise their English. (វត្តថ្មី; admission free; ⏱6am-6pm)

Wat Preah Prohm Roth
BUDDHIST TEMPLE

15 ◉ MAP P46, G5

A traditional Buddhist temple in the heart of Siem Reap, this is

The History of Siem Reap

Siem Reap was little more than a village when French explorers discovered Angkor in the 19th century. With the return of Angkor to Cambodian – or should that be French – control in 1907, Siem Reap began to grow, absorbing the first wave of tourists. The Grand Hotel d'Angkor opened its doors in 1932 and the temples of Angkor remained one of Asia's leading draws until the late 1960s, luring luminaries such as Charlie Chaplin and Jackie Kennedy. With the advent of war and the Khmer Rouge, Siem Reap entered a long slumber from which it only began to awaken in the mid-1990s.

the easiest one to explore for the casual visitor. (Wat Prohm Roth St; admission free; ⏰6am-6pm)

Bayon Information Centre   MUSEUM

16 ◎ MAP P42, E2

This exhibition introduces the visitor to the history of the Khmer empire and the restoration projects around Angkor through a series of short films and displays. Set in the beautiful Japanese Team for Safeguarding Angkor (JSA) compound, it's considerably cheaper than the Angkor National Museum, although there is no statuary on display. (☏092 165083; www.angkor-jsa.org/bic; US$2; ⏰8am-4pm Tue, Wed & Fri-Sun)

Cambodian Cultural Village   CULTURAL CENTRE

17 ◎ MAP P42, A2

It may be kitsch, it may be kooky, but it's very popular with Cambodians and provides a diversion for families travelling with children. This is the Cambodian Cultural Village, which tries to represent all of Cambodia in a whirlwind tour of recreated houses and villages. The visit begins with a wax museum and includes homes of the Cham, Chinese, Kreung and Khmer people, as well as miniature replicas of landmark buildings in Cambodia.

There are dance shows and performances throughout the day, but it still doesn't add up to much for most foreign visitors, unless they have the kids in tow. It's located about midway between Siem Reap and the airport. (ភូមិវប្បធម៌កម្ពុជា; ☏063-963836; www.cambodiancul turalvillage.com; Airport Rd; adult/child under 1.1m US$9/free; ⏰8am-7pm; 👫)

Miniature Replicas of Angkor's Temples   SCULPTURE

18 ◎ MAP P44, E2

One of the more quirky places in town is the garden of local master sculptor Dy Proeung, which houses miniature replicas of Angkor Wat, the Bayon, Banteay Srei and other temples. It is the bluffer's way to get an aerial shot of Angkor without chartering a helicopter, although the astute might question the presence of oversized insects in the shot.

There is also a display of scale miniatures at Preah Ko temple (p135). (គុំចម្លងចម្លាក់ប្រាសាទ អង្គរវត្ត; 16 Slokram District; US$2; ⏱9am-5pm)

Eating

Marum   INTERNATIONAL $

🔞 19 ❌ MAP P44, E2

Set in a delightful wooden house with a spacious garden, Marum serves up lots of vegetarian and seafood dishes, plus some mouth-watering desserts. Menu highlights include beef with red ants and chilli stir-fry, and mini crocodile burgers. Marum is part of the Tree Alliance group of training restaurants; the experience is a must.

There's a great shop here too, and the whole place is extremely kid-friendly. (☎017 363284; www.marum-restaurant.org; Wat Polanka area; mains US$3.25-6.75; ⏱11am-10.30pm; 🛜🖉🏠)

Pot & Pan Restaurant   CAMBODIAN $

20 ❌ MAP P44, B6

One of the best-value Khmer restaurants in the downtown area, Pot & Pan specialises in well-presented, authentic dishes at affordable prices. The menu includes spicy soups and subtle salads, and rice is beautifully served in a lotus leaf. Some of the cheapest pizzas in town are, somewhat surpris-ingly, also available here. (☎017 970780; www.thepotandpanrestaurant.com; Stung Thmei Rd; meals US$2-5; ⏱10am-10pm; 🛜)

Bloom Cafe   CAFE $

21 ❌ MAP P46, D2

Cupcakes are elevated to an art form at this elegant cafe, with beautifully presented creations available in a rotating array of 48 flavours. Creative coffees, teas and juices are also on offer. Profits assist Cambodian women in vocational training. (www.bloomcakes.org; St 6; cupcakes US$1.50; ⏱10am-5pm Mon-Sat; 🛜)

Gelato Lab   ICE CREAM $

22 ❌ MAP P46, C5

The great ice cream scooped up here is thanks to the state-of-the-art equipment, all-natural ingredients and – most importantly – plenty of passion courtesy of the Italian owner. Also pours some of the best hand-roasted coffee in town. (www.facebook.com/gelatolabsiemreap; 109 Alley West; 1/2 scoops US$1.50/2.50; ⏱9am-11pm; 🛜)

Road 60 Night Market   MARKET $

23 ❌ MAP P42, H2

For a slice of local life, head to the Road 60 Night Market located on the side of the road near the main Angkor ticket checkpoint. Stallholders set up each night, and it's a great place to sample local Cambodian snacks, including the full range of deep-fried insects, barbecue dishes such as quail, and plenty of cheap beer. (Rd 60; snacks US$1-4; ⏱4-11pm)

Little Red Fox

CAFE $

24 ✖ MAP P46, F2

This foxy little cafe is incredibly popular with long-term residents in Siem Reap, who swear that the regionally sourced Feel Good coffee is the best in town. Add to that designer breakfasts, bagels, salads, creative juices and air-con and it's easy to while away some time here. The slick upstairs wing is popular with the laptop crowd. (www.thelittleredfoxespresso.com; Hup Guan St; dishes US$2-8; ⏱7am-5pm Thu-Tue; ❄)

Sister Srey Cafe

CAFE $

25 ✖ MAP P46, E6

Sister Srey, a funky and fun cafe on the riverfront near Psar Chaa, offers an ambitious breakfast menu, including eggs bene-delicious, that is perfect after a sunrise at the temples. Lunch is Western food with a creative twist, including burgers, wraps and salads. (www.sistersreycafe.com; 200 Pokambor Ave; mains US$3-6; ⏱7am-6pm Tue-Sun; ✏)

Peace Cafe

VEGETARIAN $

26 ✖ MAP P44, F1

This popular garden cafe serves affordable vegetarian meals, while healthy drinks include a tempting selection of vegetable juices. A focal point for community activities, it hosts twice-daily yoga sessions and twice-weekly Khmer classes and monk chanting. (www.peacecafeangkor.org; Siem Reap River Rd East; mains US$2.50-4.50; ⏱7am-9pm; ✏)

Banllé Vegetarian Restaurant

VEGETARIAN $

27 ✖ MAP P46, H6

Set in a traditional wooden house with its own organic vegetable garden, this is a great place for a healthy bite. The menu offers a blend of international and Cambodian dishes, including a vegetable *amok* and zesty fruit and vegetable shakes. (www.banlle-vegetarian.com; St 26; dishes US$2-4; ⏱11am-9.30pm Wed-Mon; 🛜✏)

Psar Chaa

CAMBODIAN $

When it comes to cheap Khmer eats, Psar Chaa market (see 125 🔒 Map p46, D6) has plenty of food stalls on the northwestern side, all with signs and menus in English. These are atmospheric places for a local meal at local-ish prices. Some dishes are on display, others are freshly wok-fried to order, but most are wholesome and filling. (mains US$1.50-4; ⏱7am-9pm)

Khmer Kitchen Restaurant

CAMBODIAN $

28 ✖ MAP P46, D5

Can't get no (culinary) satisfaction? Then follow in the footsteps of Sir Mick Jagger and try this popular place, which offers an affordable selection of Khmer and

GAGLIA/SHUTTERSTOCK ©

Restaurant on Pub St

Thai favourites, including zesty curries. It expanded massively in 2017 and now covers a whole block of classic colonial-era buildings. (📞012 763468; www.khmerkitchens.com; The Alley; mains US$2-5; ⏰11am-10pm; 🛜)

Bugs Cafe
CAMBODIAN $

29 ❌ MAP P46, B1

Cambodians were onto insects long before the food scientists started bugging us about their merits. Choose from a veritable feast of crickets, water bugs, silkworms and spiders. Tarantula doughnuts, pan-fried scorpions, snakes – you won't forget this menu in a hurry. (📞017 764560; www.bugs-cafe.com; Angkor Night Market St; dishes US$2-8; ⏰5-11pm; 🛜)

The Hive Siem Reap
CAFE $

30 ❌ MAP P46, G2

This place has generated a real buzz among foreign residents in Siem Reap thanks to its creative coffees, jam-jar juices and healthy open sandwiches, such as smashed avocado or smoked salmon on rye. Try an espresso martini if you like your coffee with a kick. (www.facebook.com/thehive.siemreap; Psar Kandal St; dishes US$2-6; ⏰7am-6pm; ❄️🛜)

New Leaf Book Cafe
CAFE $

31 ❌ MAP P46, F5

The profits from this cafe and secondhand bookshop go towards supporting NGOs working in Siem Reap Province. The menu includes some home favourites, an Italian twist and some local Cambodian specials. (http://newleafeatery.com; near Psar Chaa; mains US$3-6; ⏰7.30am-10pm)

Pages Cafe
CAFE $

32 🍴 MAP P44, D6

This hip little hideaway is no longer so hidden with popular Viroth's Hotel now opposite. Exposed brickwork and designer decor make it a good place to linger over the excellent breakfasts or tapas. On Saturday they offer an outdoor grill with wine and pool access. Rooms also available. (☎092 966812; www.pages-siemreap.com; St 24; dishes US$2-6; ⏰6am-10pm; 🛜)

Common Grounds
CAFE $

33 🍴 MAP P46, G2

This sophisticated international cafe, akin to Starbucks, has great coffee, homemade cakes, light bites, and free wi-fi and internet terminals. Offers free computer classes and English classes for Cambodians, and supports good causes. (www.commongroundscafes.org; 719 St 14; light meals US$3-5; ⏰7am-10pm; 🛜)

Blue Pumpkin
CAFE $

34 🍴 MAP P46, E5

This is the original branch of an expanding local chain. Venture upstairs for a world of white minimalism, with beds to lounge on and free wi-fi. The menu includes light bites, great sandwiches, filling specials and divine shakes. The homemade ice cream comes in some exotic flavours.

There are several additional locations around town (see website), including one at the airport. (www.bluepumpkin.asia; Pithnou St; mains US$3-8; ⏰6am-10pm; ❄🛜)

Wat Damnak BBQs
BARBECUE $

35 🍴 MAP P44, C6

Located opposite the venerable Wat Dam Nak, these local barbecue restaurants are popular for barbecued beef, other local meats and lake fish. They also double as beer emporiums and turn out some of the cheapest draught in town. (Wat Dam Nak St; mains US$2-5; ⏰11am-11pm)

Pho Yong
VIETNAMESE $

36 🍴 MAP P44, E1

Pho Yong is a noodle soup emporium specialising in the national dish of Vietnam, a steaming bow of noodle soup with beef or chicken. Stock up (and it's good stock) before or after a visit to the Angkor National Museum across the road. (☎078 207720; Charles de Gaulle Blvd; pho from US$2; ⏰6.30am-10pm; 🛜)

Lelawadee Restaurant
THAI $

37 🍴 MAP P44, B7

One of the best Thai restaurants in Siem Reap, this is where the Bangkok crowd make for when they need a spicy fix. The Thai owners whip up authentic recipes on the riverside, including *tom yum kong* and spicy papaya salad. (☎063-636 4761; www.lelawadeerestaurant.com; 311 Siem Reap River Rd East; mains US$3-8; ⏰10am-10pm; 🛜)

Father's Restaurant CAMBODIAN $

38 🍴 MAP P44, A5

An authentic little Khmer eatery on popular Sok San Rd, Father's Restaurant offers all the favourite flavours from Cambodia and China, including a tender beef *lok lak* and zesty deep-fried pork ribs with pepper. (☎ 012 948248; www.fathersrestaurant.com; Sok San Rd; meals US$2.50-6; ⏰ 10am-10pm Mon-Sat; 🛜)

Curry Walla INDIAN $

39 🍴 MAP P44, C4

For good-value Indian food, this place is hard to beat. The *thalis* (set meals) are a bargain and the owner, long-time resident Ranjit, knows his share of spicy specials from the subcontinent. (Sivatha St; mains US$2-6; ⏰ 10.30am-11pm)

The Glasshouse ICE CREAM $

40 🍴 MAP P44, C4

Velvety ice creams including white chocolate and tangy sorbets. (www.facebook.com/theglasshousedelipatisserie; Park Hyatt, Sivatha St; cones US$2; ⏰ 6am-10pm; 🛜)

Moloppor Cafe JAPANESE, INTERNATIONAL $

41 🍴 MAP P44, D5

One of the cheapest deals in Siem Reap, Moloppor Cafe serves up Japanese, Asian and Italian dishes at almost giveaway prices for what is a real restaurant. Nice location offering river views. (www.facebook.com/molopporcafeofficial; Siem Reap River Rd East; mains US$1.50-5; ⏰ 10am-11pm; 🛜)

Swenson's Ice Cream ICE CREAM $

42 🍴 MAP P46, F5

One of America's favourites has become one of Siem Reap's favourites. Located in the Angkor Trade Centre. (Pokambor Ave; cones US$1.25; ⏰ 9am-9pm)

Angkor Market SUPERMARKET $

43 🍴 MAP P44, C3

The best all-round supermarket in town, this place has a steady supply of international treats. (Sivatha St; ⏰ 8am-9pm)

Thai Huot SUPERMARKET $

44 🍴 MAP P46, G1

Easily the most modern supermarket in Siem Reap, with tons of French and other imported products. (Tep Vong St; ⏰ 8am-10pm)

Mie Cafe CAMBODIAN, INTERNATIONAL $$

45 🍴 MAP P42, E3

An impressive Cambodian eatery offering a fusion take on traditional flavours. It is set in a wooden house just off the road to Angkor and offers a gourmet set menu for US$24. Dishes include everything from succulent marinated pork ribs to squid-ink ravioli. (☎ 069 999096; www.miecafe-siemreap.com; near Angkor Conservation; mains US$4-8; ⏰ 11am-2pm & 5.30-10pm Wed-Mon)

MICHAEL HEAULT/GETTY IMAGES ©

Khmer stir fry

Haven
FUSION $$

46  MAP P44, E7

A culinary haven indeed. Dine here for the best of East meets West; the fish fillet with green mango is particularly zesty. Proceeds go towards helping young adult orphans make the step from institution to employment. (☏078-342404; www.haven-cambodia.com; Chocolate Rd, Wat Dam Nak area; mains US$6-8; ⏰11.30am-2.30pm & 5.30-9.30pm Mon-Sat, closed Aug; 🛜)

Spoons Cafe
CAMBODIAN $$

47 MAP P44, D7

This excellent contemporary-Cambodian restaurant supports local community EGBOK (Everything's Gonna Be OK), which offers education, training and employment opportunities in the hospitality sector. The menu includes some original flavours such as *trey saba* (whole mackerel) with coconut-turmeric rice, tiger-prawn curry and *tuk kroeung*, a pungent local fish-based broth. Original cocktails are shaken, not stirred. (☏076 277 6667; www.spoonscambodia.org; Bamboo Rd; mains US$5.50-8; ⏰11.30am-10pm Tue-Sun; 🛜)

Chanrey Tree
CAMBODIAN $$

48 MAP P46, G3

Chanrey Tree is all about contemporary Khmer cuisine, combining a stylish setting with expressive presentation, while retaining the essentials of traditional Cambodian cooking. Try the eggplant with pork ribs or grilled stuffed frog. (☏063-767997; www.chanreytree.

com; Pokambor Ave; mains US$5-12; ⏱11am-2pm & 5.30-10pm; ❄ 🎅)

Sugar Palm
CAMBODIAN $$

49 🍴 MAP P44, E6

Recently relocated to the east bank, the Sugar Palm is a popular place to sample traditional flavours infused with herbs and spices, including delicious *char kreung* (curried lemongrass) dishes. Owner Kethana showed celebrity chef Gordon Ramsay how to prepare *amok*. (www.thesugarpalm.com; St 27; mains US$5-9; ⏱11.30am-3pm & 5.30-10.30pm Mon-Sat; 🎅)

Le Malraux
FRENCH $$

50 🍴 MAP P46, E5

Recently relocated to the network of alleys east of Psar Chaa, Le Malraux is one of the best French restaurants in Siem Reap. Eat or drink inside at the bar or alfresco in the street. Meals includes a superb *pavê* of *boeuf* and succulent fish. (☎012 332584; http://le-malraux-siem-reap.fr; mains US$5-15; ⏱10am-11pm; 🎅)

Mamma Shop
ITALIAN $$

51 🍴 MAP P46, E2

A compact menu of terrific homemade pasta is the signature of this bright, friendly Italian corner bistro in the up-and-coming Kandal Village district. Add a selection of *piadina romagnola* (stuffed flatbread) pizza, a nice wine list and delicious desserts, and this place is highly recommended. (www.facebook.com/mammashop.italian.restaurant; Hup

Guan St; mains US$5-9; ⏱11.30am-10.30pm Mon-Sat; ❄ 🎅)

Mahob
CAMBODIAN $$

52 🍴 MAP P42, E3

The Cambodian word for food is *mahob,* and at this restaurant it is delicious. Set in a traditional wooden house with a contemporary twist, they take the same approach to cuisine as they do to decor, serving up dishes such as caramelised pork shank with ginger and black pepper, or wok-fried local beef with red tree ants. Cooking classes available. (☎063-966986; www.mahobkhmer.com; near Angkor Conservation; dishes US$3.50-15; ⏱11am-11pm)

Olive
FRENCH $$

53 🍴 MAP P46, F5

The crisp white linens and air-con beckon diners into this French restaurant hidden away down a side street near the Old Market. The menu includes a good range of Gallic classics, including rack of lamb and pork tenderloin. Save space for the desserts or a cheese platter. (☎012 244196; www.facebook.com/olivecuisinedesaison; off Siem Reap River Rd West; mains US$5-15; ⏱11am-10.30pm; ❄ 🎅)

Il Forno
ITALIAN $$

54 🍴 MAP P46, C4

Aficionados of fine Italian cuisine will be delighted to know that there is, as the name suggests, a full-blown brick oven in this cosy little trattoria. The menu includes fresh antipasti, authentic pizzas and some home-cooked Italian dishes. (☎063-763380; http://ilforno. restaurant; The Lane; mains US$5-15; ⏱11am-11pm; 🛜)

Flow

FUSION $$

55 🍽 MAP P46, H5

This chic, contemporary space is earning a local following for its creative cuisine that mixes the best of East and West. Starters include octopus carpaccio while mains include tender beef cheek and pan-fried sea bass. The wine list is extensive so go with the Flow! (☎012 655285; www.facebook. com/flowfoodandwine; St 26; dishes US$5-12; ⏱5-11pm; ❄🛜)

Vibe Cafe

VEGAN $$

56 🍽 MAP P46, G2

This new vegan spot promises raw organically sourced superfood bowls and cleansing juices such as the cashew, date, Himalayan salt, vanilla bean and Ayurvedic spices concoction. If that sounds too healthy for you after partying on Pub St, try the excellent vegan desserts such as raspberry cheesecake and chocolate-ganache truffle. (☎069 937900; www.vibecafeasia. com; 715 Hup Guan St; mains US$3-7; ⏱7.30am-6pm; ❄🛜🍴)

Cambodian BBQ

BARBECUE $$

57 🍽 MAP P46, D5

Crocodile, snake, ostrich and kangaroo meat add an exotic twist

to the traditional *phnom pleung* (hill of fire) grills. Cambodian BBQ has spawned half a dozen or more copycats in the surrounding streets, many of which offer discount specials. (www.restaurant-siemreap.com; The Alley; mains US$5-10; ⏱11am-11pm; 🛜)

Touich

CAMBODIAN $$

58 🍽 MAP P42, F3

Hidden away but worth the search, this traditional Khmer restaurant is set in the backstreet suburbs of Wat Preah Inkosei. The menu includes regional specialities and seafood such as Mekong prawns and Koh Kong red snapper. Check the blog for directions to avoid getting lost. (http://the-touich-restaurant-bar.blogspot.com; mains US$2.50-8; ⏱6-10.30pm; 🛜)

Village Cafe

FRENCH $$

59 🍽 MAP P46, F1

The Village Cafe is a lively little bistro that has one of the longer bars in Siem Reap. Drop in for tapas, wholesome gastropub grub and a glass of wine or four to wash it all down. Regular DJ events at weekends draw a crowd. (☎092 305401; www.facebook.com/villagecafecambodia; 586 Tep Vong St; mains US$5-15; ⏱5pm-late Mon-Sat; ❄🛜)

FCC Angkor

INTERNATIONAL $$

60 🍽 MAP P44, D3

This landmark building draws people in from the riverside thanks to a reflective pool, torchlit dining and a garden bar. Inside, the colonial-chic atmosphere continues with lounge chairs and an open kitchen turning out a range of Asian and international food. (☏ 063-760280; www.fcccambodia.com; Pokambor Ave; mains US$5-15; ⏰ 7am-midnight; 🛜)

Cafe Central
INTERNATIONAL $$

61 🍴 MAP P46, C6

Cafe Central occupies a handsome building overlooking Psar Chaa. The menu is East meets West, with marinated ribs, fish and chips, authentic pizzas plus some Cambodian faves such as *amok* fish and vegetable curry. The coffee is highly regarded thanks to the La Marzocco coffee machine. (☏ 017 692997; www.facebook.com/cafecentralsiemreap; Psar Chaa; meals US$4-9; ⏰ 7am-10pm; 🛜)

Le Tigre de Papier
INTERNATIONAL $$

62 🍴 MAP P46, D5

One of the best all-rounders in Siem Reap, the popular Paper Tiger serves up authentic Khmer food, great Italian dishes and a selection of favourites from most other corners of the globe. It conveniently offers frontage on both Pub St and the Alley; the latter is generally a lot quieter. (www.letigre depapier.com; Pub St; mains US$2-9; ⏰ 24hr; 🛜 🍴)

Chamkar
VEGETARIAN $$

63 🍴 MAP P46, D5

The name translates as 'farm' and the ingredients must be coming from a pretty impressive organic vegetable supplier given

Food stall

the creative dishes on the menu here. Asian flavours dominate and include dishes such as vegetable kebabs in black pepper sauce and stuffed pumpkin. (📞 092 733150; The Alley; mains US$4-8; 🕙 11am-10.30pm Mon-Sat, 5-10.30pm Sun; 🛜 🍴)

Amok CAMBODIAN $$

64 ✖ MAP P46, D5

The name pays homage to Cambodia's national dish, *amok* (or *amoc*; baked fish), and this is indeed a fine place to try baked fish curry in banana leaf or, better still, an *amok* tasting platter with four varieties. It is in the heart of the Alley. (www.angkorw.com; The Alley; mains US$4-9; 🕙 10am-11pm; 🛜)

Le Jardin des Délices INTERNATIONAL $$

65 ✖ MAP P42, A2

Enjoy high-end standards at an affordable price with a three-course lunch of Asian and Western food prepared by students training in the culinary arts. It also runs a 'Khmer Food Lovers' cooking class. (📞 063-963673; www.ecolepauldu brule.org; Paul Dubrule Hotel & Tourism School; NH6; set lunch US$15; 🕙 noon-2pm Tue-Fri; ❄ 🛜)

Siem Reap Brewpub INTERNATIONAL $$

66 ✖ MAP P44, D4

Designer dining meets designer brewing. Set in an open-plan villa, the menu is international

fusion, including everything from light bites and tapas to gourmet meals. The beer comes in several flavours, including blonde, golden, amber and dark, and a sampling platter is available. (📞 080 888555; www.siemreapbrewpub.asia; St 5; meals US$4-15; 🕙 11am-11pm)

Siem Reap Food Co-op CAFE $$

67 ✖ MAP P44, E7

Promoting healthy, organic, locally sourced food is the mission of the Siem Reap Food Co-op, which doubles as a wholesaler as well as a popular garden cafe set in a traditional wooden house. The menu features some international classics such as the Luxemburger and falafel, plus fusion Cambodian dishes including 'fall off the bone ribs' and stir-fried mango prawns.

Weekends see some fun promotions such as 'sacred sangria' for US$1 a glass. (📞 015 932620; www. facebook.com/siemreapfoodcoop; Chocolate Rd; meals US$4-8; 🕙 9am-6pm; 🛜)

Red Piano ASIAN, INTERNATIONAL $$

68 ✖ MAP P46, C5

Strikingly set in a restored colonial-era gem, Red Piano has a big balcony for watching the action unfold below. The menu has a reliable selection of Asian and international food, all at decent prices. Former celebrity guest Angelina Jolie has a cocktail named in her honour. (📞 063-963240; www. redpianocambodia.com; Pub St; mains US$3-10; 🛜)

Soup Dragon ASIAN, INTERNATIONAL $$

69 ❌ MAP P46, D5

This three-level restaurant in the heart of the action is a fun place to come for authentic Vietnamese food, with roll-your-own *banh xeo* (pancake wraps) and other DIY faves on the menu, plus Italian flavours.

Wander up to the lively rooftop bar, where 7% of proceeds go to the Angkor Children's Hospital – so you're helping someone else's liver, if not your own. (Pub St; mains US$2-10; ☾6am-midnight; 📶)

Burger Gourmand BURGERS $$

70 ❌ MAP P44, B5

This French-run burger joint really is gourmand, thanks to home-made buns and a list of patties that includes beef, pork, duck, chicken, fish and vegetarian. The toppings list is even more eclectic and includes such delicacies as foie gras. Set meals offer a good-value meal with drink and dessert. (📞087 463640; www.facebook.com/burger.gourmand.siemreap; Sok San Rd; meals US$5-15; ☾11am-3pm & 5-9.30pm Tue-Sun; ❄📶)

Jungle Burger INTERNATIONAL $$

71 ❌ MAP P46, H5

There are more than 10 types of burger on offer here, including the huge Burg Kalifa burger, plus pizzas, foot-long subs and Kiwi comfort food such as homemade pies thanks to the NZ owner. It doubles as a small sports bar with a popular pool table. (📞098 293400; www.facebook.com/jungleburgersiemreap; St 26; burgers US$2.50-10; ☾11am-11pm; 📶)

Temple Coffee & Bakery INTERNATIONAL $$

72 ❌ MAP P46, H4

This huge place is a bakery, restaurant and cocktail lounge mash-up. Downstairs there are vintage motorbikes and inviting cakes, or continue up to the rooftop bar with a pool (open from 5pm), a popular romantic retreat for young Cambodians. The menu is surprisingly affordable given the glamour; it includes tasty pastas, light bites and elegantly presented Cambodian dishes. (www.facebook.com/templebakery; Siem Reap River Rd East; dishes US$3-12; ☾6am-midnight; ❄📶)

King's Road INTERNATIONAL $$

73 ❌ MAP P44, D6

King's Road is an upmarket dining destination on the east bank of the Siem Reap River. You can browse the daily Made in Cambodia (p75) community market of craft stalls, then choose from about 10 restaurants set in beautiful traditional Cambodian wooden buildings. It hasn't been as successful as hoped, however, so it feels more like a market than dining destination.

Dining choices include Cambodian, Asian, fusion and international. (https://kingsroadangkor.com; Siem Reap River Rd East; ☾7am-midnight; 📶)

Kanell
INTERNATIONAL $$

74  MAP P44, E7

Set in a handsome Khmer villa on the edge of town, Kanell offers extensive gardens and a swimming pool (free with US$5 spend) for those seeking to dine and unwind. The menu includes French-accented dishes, plus some Cambodian favourites. (☎077 207100; www.kanellrestaurant. com; 7 Makara St; mains US$4-13; ☺10am-10pm; ☎)

Madame Butterfly
ASIAN $$

75 MAP P42, B3

This traditional wooden house has been sumptuously decorated with fine silks and billowing drapes. The lovely atmosphere is sometimes dampened, however,

by the sheer number of tour groups who come to sample the Asian and Khmer cuisine, which includes caramalised pork and red chicken curry. (☎063-966281; www.madamebutterfly-restaurant. com; Airport Rd; mains US$4-10; ☺10am-11pm; ☎)

Por Cuisine
CAMBODIAN $$

76 MAP P42, F6

A stylish contemporary restaurant, Por Cuisine offers a wide selection of Asian and international dishes, including the best of Cambodian flavours. The nightly classical dance show is one of the more sophisticated on offer and is an affordable way to get a cultural fix in Siem Reap. (☎063-967797; www. porcuisine.com; dishes US$3.50-18; ☺10.30am-10.30pm; ❄☎)

Fruit juice stall

INGE HOGENBIJL/SHUTTERSTOCK ©

Kuriosity Kafe
INTERNATIONAL $$

77 ⊗ MAP P46, A5

Impressively set over three floors, this place has a quirky and kitsch look that stands out from the pack in up-and-coming Sok San Rd. The menu blends home comfort food such as sandwiches and wraps with authentic Khmer food, including an aromatic chicken curry. (☎063-963240; http://kuriositykafe. com; Sok San Rd; dishes US$4-12; ⊙10am-midnight; ☎)

Dakshin's
INDIAN $$

78 ⊗ MAP P46, D4

Arguably the best of Siem Reap's numerous Indian restaurants, Dakshin's serves up a delicious butter chicken alongside the highlights of northern and southern cuisine. Such is their confidence in their subcontinental skills that they have an open-plan kitchen. (☎012 808011; Pithnou St; mains US$2-8; ⊙11am-3pm & 5-11pm; ☎)

Dakida
KOREAN $$

79 ⊗ MAP P44, C3

There are other things on the menu, but the main draw is the all-you-can-eat dinner set – unlimited volcano egg pot soup, sides, and pork belly strips seared right at your table. (Oum Khun St; mains US$5-10; ⊙5pm-2am; ✳☎)

Little Italy
ITALIAN $$

80 ⊗ MAP P46, C6

This elegant Italian restaurant is much more affordable than its

sophisticated exterior might suggest. As well as wood-fired pizzas, the menu includes a wide range of homemade pastas and imported Italian cuts. (☎012 315911; Alley West; mains US$4-12; ⊙11am-11pm; ☎)

Viva
MEXICAN $$

81 ⊗ MAP P46, E5

Spice up your life with Mexican food and margaritas at this long-running place, strategically situated opposite Psar Chaa. There's a guesthouse located above. (www. ivivasiemreap.com; Pithnou St; mains US$2.50-12.50; ⊙7am-11.30pm; ☎)

L'Oasi Italiana
ITALIAN $$

82 ⊗ MAP P42, F3

L'Oasi Italiana really is something of an oasis, hidden away in a forest near Wat Preah Inkosei. Expats swear by the gnocchi and homemade pasta, including ravioli with porcini mushrooms, plus wood-fired pizzas. (www.oasiitaliana. com; Siem Reap River Rd East; pizzas US$5-9, mains US$5-17; ⊙6-10pm Mon, 11am-2pm & 6-10pm Tue-Sun; ☎)

Belmiro's Pizzas & Subs
INTERNATIONAL $$

83 ⊗ MAP P46, D4

No prizes for guessing what's served here. They rightly claim to serve the biggest pizzas in town, conveniently sold by the slice if you can't cope with a whole pie. Regular specials include anything from an original French dip sandwich to big burritos. (☎095 331875;

www.facebook.com/belmiros.pizza; St 7; pizzas US$3-12; ⊙noon-midnight)

Japanese Restaurant Genkiya
JAPANESE $$

84 ⊗ MAP P44, C2

There are lots of Japanese restaurants in Siem Reap these days, but Genkiya is noteworthy for its bargain set lunches (US$7). Choose from a variety of sets, including grilled mackerel, sashimi, shrimp and salmon, fried chicken or tempura. (☎063-967978; Airport Rd; meals US$6-18; ⊙11.30am-2pm & 6-10pm)

Cuisine Wat Damnak
CAMBODIAN $$$

85 ⊗ MAP P44, E8

Set in a traditional wooden house is this highly regarded restaurant from Siem Reap celeb chef Joannès Rivière. The menu delivers the ultimate contemporary Khmer dining experience. Seasonal set menus focus on market-fresh ingredients and change weekly; vegetarian options are available with advance notice. (☎077 347762; www.cuisinewatdamnak.com; Wat Dam Nak area; 5-/6-course menu US$24/28; ⊙6.30-10.30pm Tue-Sat, last orders 9.30pm)

Embassy
CAMBODIAN $$$

86 ⊗ MAP P46, H6

Part of the King's Rd village, Embassy is all about Khmer gastronomy, offering an evolving menu that changes with the seasons. Under the supervision of the Kimsan twins,

who studied with Michelin-starred chef Régis Marcon, this is Khmer cuisine prepared at its most creative. (☎089 282911; www.embassy-restaurant.com; St 27, King's Rd; set menus from US$28; ⊙6pm-11pm)

Hashi
JAPANESE $$$

87 ⊗ MAP P44, D5

A big, bright and boisterous sushi parlour. Navigate through the SUVs parked outside, waddle up to the fish-shaped sushi bar and order the likes of spicy tuna rolls, chirashi sushi bowls or, for the fish averse, wagyu beef tenderloin. (www.thehashi.com; Wat Bo Rd; meals US$15-50; ⊙11am-3pm & 6-11pm; ❄☎)

Drinking

Asana Wooden House
BAR

88 ☕ MAP P46, D4

This is a traditional Cambodian countryside home dropped into the backstreets of Siem Reap, which makes for an atmospheric place to drink. Lounge on *kapok*-filled rice sacks while sipping a classic cocktail made with infused rice wine. Khmer cocktail classes (US$15 per person) with Sombai spirits are available. (www.asana-cambodia.com; The Lane; ⊙11am-late; ☎)

Miss Wong
BAR

89 ☕ MAP P46, D4

Miss Wong carries you back to chic 1920s Shanghai. The cocktails are a draw here, making it a cool place to while away an evening, and there's a menu offering dim

ARCON THAEWCHATTURAT/ALAMY STOCK PHOTO ©

Miss Wong

sum. Gay-friendly and extremely popular with the well-heeled expat crowd. (www.misswong.net; The Lane; ⊙6pm-1am; 📶)

Laundry Bar BAR

90 🚇 MAP P46, E5

One of the most chilled, chic bars in town thanks to low lighting and discerning decor. This is the place to come for electronica and ambient sounds; it heaves on weekends or when guest DJs crank up the volume. Happy hour until 9pm. (www.facebook.com/laundry.bar.3; St 9; ⊙4pm-late; 📶)

Soul Train Reggae Bar BAR

91 🚇 MAP P46, F4

One of the most lively late-night spots in town, this bar is tucked away down the side street that passes Wat Preah Prohm Roth, so hopefully the reggae beats are subtle enough not to disturb the monks. Great tunes, cheap drinks and a party atmosphere that is more chilled than Pub St. (www.facebook.com/soultrainreggaebar; 35 New St; ⊙5pm-late)

Picasso BAR

92 🚇 MAP P46, C6

This tiny tapas bar in the Alley West area is a convivial spot for a bit of over-the-counter banter. With only a dozen or so stools, expect spillover into the street – especially once the cheap sangria, worldly wines and cheap Tiger bottles start flowing. (Alley West; ⊙5pm-late; 📶)

The Harbour
BAR

93 MAP P44, A7

Shiver me timbers, this self-styled 'pirate tavern' is a loveable bar housed in an atmospheric wooden house in Stung Thmei. Upstairs are cocktails, booze aplenty and regular open mic, comedy and other events; downstairs is the famous Lex Roulor Tattoo Studio. Just make sure you don't get so drunk you wake up with an unplanned inking. (www.theharbour siemreap.com; Stung Thmei St; 10am-1am;)

Beatnik Bar
BAR

94 MAP P46, C5

A hip little bar on the corner of the Alley, it is just far enough away from Pub St not to be drowned out by the nightly battle of the bars. Cheap drinks, friendly staff and a convivial crowd add up to a great pit stop. (www.facebook.com/beatniksiemreap; The Alley; 9.30am-1.30am;)

Angkor What?
BAR

95 MAP P46, D5

Siem Reap's original bar claims to have been promoting irresponsible drinking since 1998. The happy hour (to 9pm) lightens the mood for later when everyone's bouncing along to dance anthems, sometimes on the tables, sometimes under them. (www.facebook.com/theangkorwhatbar; Pub St; 5pm-late;)

X Bar
BAR

96 MAP P46, B5

One of *the* late-night spots in town, X Bar draws revellers for the witching hour when other places are closing up. Early-evening movies on the big screen, pool tables and even a skateboard pipe – take a breath test first! (www.facebook.com/Xbar. Asia; Sivatha St; 4pm-sunrise;)

Barcode
GAY

97 MAP P46, G4

A superstylin' gay bar that's metrosexual friendly. The cocktails here are worth the stop, as is the regular drag show at 9.30pm. Happy hour runs from 5pm to 7pm daily. (www.barcodesiemreap.com; Wat Preah Prohm Roth St; 5pm-late;)

Menaka Speakeasy Lounge
COCKTAIL BAR

98 MAP P46, E6

A cultured speakeasy cocktail bar has arrived in Siem Reap. Downstairs is a cafe by day and upstairs is a hidden bar by night. The artwork pays homage to the golden years of Cambodia's music and film from the 1960s and the creative cocktails are available two-for-one from 6pm to 8pm. (www.menakalounge.asia; 275 Pithnou St; 8.30am-1am;)

Score!
SPORTS BAR

99 MAP P46, B5

Having expanded from Phnom Penh to Temple Town, Score! commands the entrance to Sok San

Rd, beckoning sports fans with an inviting open plan and ginormous two-storey screen. (www.scorekh. com; 12 Sok San Rd; ⏰8am-midnight Sun-Thu, to 2am Fri & Sat)

The Republic   BAR

100 🚇 MAP P44, D8

A new bar from the team at Siem Reap Food Co-op, this is a great place for creative cocktails, weekend DJs or bands, and regular film screenings. The wooden house is the centrepiece of a landscaped garden and there is a pool table downstairs for hustlers. (www.face book.com/therepublicsiemreap; Sala Kamreuk Rd; ⏰3pm-1am; 📶)

Hard Rock Cafe   BAR

101 🚇 MAP P44, C6

While you might not head to the Hard Rock Cafe in London or New York, it is well worth making the diversion across the bridge from the Old Market to catch the live band here. They bang out anthems from the 1960s to the '90s, ranging from the Rolling Stones to the Red Hot Chilli Peppers. (📞063-963964; www.hardrock.com/cafes/angkor; King's Rd; ⏰11am-midnight; 📶)

Home Cocktail   BAR

102 🚇 MAP P46, D3

Surely a leading candidate for the cheapest cocktail bar in town with drinks starting at US$1.50, this place is noteworthy as one of the few bars in this area that draws a genuinely mixed crowd

of Cambodians and foreigners. Reliable, inexpensive food as well. (www.facebook.com/homecocktailsrp; Pithnou St; ⏰8am-midnight; 📶)

Long's Bar   BAR

103 🚇 MAP P46, D4

A great little bolt-hole hidden away among the lanes, Long's has some creative cocktails such as pomelo and basil infusion or ginger and lemongrass mojito. Cheap beers for a proper bar, blissfully air-conditioned and no smoking inside. (www.facebook.com/longsbar siemreap; The Lane; ⏰5pm-late; 📶)

The Yellow Sub   BAR

104 🚇 MAP P46, D4

No prizes for guessing the theme here, but as far as Beatles tribute bars go, this has to be one of the best. Memorabilia plasters the walls, including signed album covers and artworks. There are multiple levels where you'll find a pool table and a 4th-floor whisky bar with single malts. Great food as well, including Beatle-themed burgers. (www.facebook.com/theyellowsub siemreap; The Lane; ⏰11am-11pm; 📶)

Linga Bar   GAY

105 🚇 MAP P46, D5

This chic gay bar attracts all comers thanks to a relaxed atmosphere, a cracking cocktail list and some ambient sounds. It was one of the first bars to set up in the Alley and it remains popular. (www.lingabar.com; The Alley; ⏰4pm-late; 📶)

Mezze Bar
BAR

106 MAP P46, C5

One of the hippest bars in Siem Reap, Mezze is located above the circus that surrounds Pub St. Ascend the stairs to a contemporary lounge-bar complete with original art, regular DJs and Sunday salsa nights. (www.mezzesiemreap.com; St 11; ◷6pm-late; 🛜)

Nest
BAR

107 MAP P44, C4

A memorable bar thanks to its sweeping sail-like shelters and stylish seating, this place has one of the most creative cocktail lists in town. Curl up in a sleigh bed and relax for the night. An impressive menu of fusion and international cuisine is available if the munchies strike. (www.nestangkor.com; Sivatha St; ◷11am-late; 🛜)

Temple Club
BAR

The only worshipping going on at this temple (see 115 ✪ Map p46, D5) is 'all hail the ale'. Things start moving early and they don't stop. It's not for the hard of hearing as the music is permanently cranked up to 11. Dangerous happy hours from 10am to 10pm. (www.facebook.com/templeclubpubstreet; Pub St; ◷10am-late; 🛜)

Temple Container Pub Zone
BEER GARDEN

108 MAP P44, A6

The first container beer garden to open its doors in Siem Reap, it looks rather like a giant set of balancing blocks, with containers creatively connected on top of each other. Cheap beers, raucous noise levels and the attached Hip Hop Nightclub where local bright young things go to dance. (www.facebook.com/templecontainerpubzone; Sok San Rd; ◷5pm-late; 🛜)

Sombai
DISTILLERY

109 MAP P46, A3

Is it drinking or is it shopping? A bit of both actually, as this booth at the Angkor Night Market sells beautiful hand-painted bottles of infused spirits and also offers free tastings from 6pm to 10pm. Choose from eight flavours including ginger and chilli or anise coffee.

Sombai spirits are also on sale in bars around Siem Reap and at the Made in Cambodia (p75) community market at King's Road. (☎095 810890; www.sombai.com; Angkor Night Market B; ◷4-11pm)

Joe to Go
CAFE

110 MAP P46, C6

If you need coffee coursing through your veins to tackle the temples, then head here. Gourmet coffees, shakes and light bites, with proceeds supporting street children. Upstairs is a small boutique supporting the associated NGO, The Global Child. (www.joetogo.org; St 9; mains US$2-5; ◷7am-9.30pm)

Entertainment

Phare the Cambodian Circus

CIRCUS

111 ⭐ MAP P42, B5

Cambodia's answer to Cirque du Soleil, Phare the Cambodian Circus is so much more than a conventional circus, with an emphasis on performance art and a subtle yet striking social message behind each production. Cambodia's leading circus, theatre and performing arts organisation, Phare Ponleu Selpak opened its big top for nightly shows in 2013 and the results are a unique form of entertainment that should be considered unmissable when staying in Siem Reap.

Several generations of performers have graduated through Phare's original Battambang campus and have gone on to perform in international shows around the world. Many of the performers have deeply moving personal stories of abuse and hardship, making their talents a triumph against the odds. An inspiring night out for adults and children alike, all proceeds are reinvested into Phare Ponleu Selpak activities. Animal lovers will be pleased to note that no animals are used in any performance. Return visitors should note that the circus has moved to the western outskirts of town and is no longer behind the Angkor National Museum. (📞015 499480; www.pharecircus.org; west end of Sok San Rd; adult/child US$18/10, premium seats US$38/18; ⏰8pm daily)

Performer at Phare the Cambodian Circus

Apsara Theatre
DANCE

112 ⭐ MAP P44, E6

The setting for this Cambodian classical-dance show is a striking wooden pavilion finished in the style of a wat. The price includes dinner. It tends to be packed to the rafters with tour groups. (📞063-963561; www.angkorvillageresort.asia/apsara-theatre; St 26; show US$27; ⏱7.30pm)

Garavek
THEATRE

113 ⭐ MAP P46, E5

Garavek is a traditional storytelling theatre that offers the chance to learn about everything from the mythical origins of the Khmer kingdom to folk tales and fables. Stories are told in English to a backdrop of traditional music. Each show lasts 45 minutes. (📞078 938132; www.garavek.com; Pithnou St; US$7; ⏱shows 6.30pm & 8pm; 🛜)

Beatocello
CLASSICAL MUSIC

114 ⭐ MAP P42, E2

Better known as Dr Beat Richner, Beatocello performs cello compositions at Jayavarman VII Children's Hospital. Entry is free, but donations are welcome as they assist the hospital in offering free medical treatment to the children of Cambodia. (www.beatocello.com; Charles de Gaulle Blvd; ⏱7.15pm Sat)

Temple Club
DANCE

115 ⭐ MAP P46, D5

Temple Club stages a free traditional-dance show upstairs nightly, providing punters order some food and drink from the very reasonably priced menu. (www.facebook.com/templeclubpubstreet; Pub St; ⏱from 7.30pm; 🛜)

Rosana Broadway
CABARET

116 ⭐ MAP P42, H5

Bringing a bit of Bangkok-style Broadway to Siem Reap, this show includes cultural dances from the region and a not-so-cultural ladyboy cabaret; ticket prices are on the high side. (📞063-769991; www.rosanabroadway.com; NH6; show US$25-45; ⏱7.30pm daily)

Smile of Angkor
DANCE

117 ⭐ MAP P42, H2

Popular with some Asian tour groups, this is the glitziest dinner-dance show in town, but in reality it doesn't live up to the hefty price tag. (📞063-655 0168; www.smileofangkor.info; show & meal US$38-48; ⏱7.15pm daily)

Shopping

Artisans Angkor
ARTS & CRAFTS

On the premises of Les Chantiers Écoles (p48) is this beautiful shop (see 1 ◉ Map p44, B6), which sells everything from stone and wood reproductions of Angkorian-era statues to household furnishings. There's also a second shop opposite Angkor Wat in the Angkor Cafe building, and outlets at Phnom Penh and Siem Reap international airports.

All profits from sales go back into funding the school and bringing more young Cambodians into the training program, which is 20% owned by the artisans themselves. (www.artisansdangkor.com; ⏱7.30am-6.30pm)

AHA Fair Trade Village

ARTS & CRAFTS

118 🔒 MAP P42, F2

For locally produced souvenirs (unlike much of the imported stuff that turns up in Psar Chaa) drop in on this handicraft market. It's a little out of the way, but there are more than 20 stalls selling a wide range of traditional items. There's a Khmer cultural show every second and fourth Saturday of the month, with extra stalls, traditional music and dancing.

Two-hour pottery classes are offered here through **Mordock Ceramics**, one of the stalls. (📱078 341454; www.aha-kh.com; Rd 60, Trang Village; ⏱10am-7pm)

Angkor Night Market

MARKET

119 🔒 MAP P46, A4

Siem Reap's original night market near Sivatha St has sprung countless copycats, but it remains the best and is well worth a browse. It's packed with stalls selling a variety of handicrafts, souvenirs and silks. In 'Night Market A' (to the south), you can catch live music at Island Bar, while adjacent 'Night Market B' has the Brick House bar.

You can also indulge in a Dr Fish massage or watch a 3D event movie (US$3) about the Khmer Rouge or the scourge of land-mines. (https://angkornightmarket. com; ⏱4pm-midnight)

Theam's House

ART

120 🔒 MAP P42, D1

After years spent helping Artisans Angkor (p48) revitalise Khmer handicrafts, Cambodian artist and designer Theam now operates his own studio of lacquer creations and artwork. Highly original, it can be tricky to find, so make sure you find a driver who knows where it is. A beautiful and creative space. (www.theamshouse.com; 25 Veal, Kokchak District; ⏱8am-7pm)

Samatoa

FASHION & ACCESSORIES

121 🔒 MAP P44, B8

Samatoa experiments in organic fibres, blending silk and cotton with lotus to create 'the most spiritual fabric in the world'. Plants such as lotus and banana have natural fibres that create a softness and texture not found in pure silk or cotton. Order tailor-made clothes to measure or visit the lotus farm to learn about the process. (www.samatoa.com; 11 Rd 63; ⏱9am-5pm Mon-Sat)

trunkh.

GIFTS & SOUVENIRS

122 🔒 MAP P46, F2

The owner here has a great eye for the quirky, stylish and original, including beautiful shirts, throw pillows, jewellery, poster art, and T's, plus some offbeat items such as genuine Cambodian water-buffalo bells. (www.trunkh.com; Hup Guan St; ⏱10am-6pm)

Spooling silk at Artisans Angkor (p72)

Soieries du Mekong
FASHION & ACCESSORIES

123 🔒 MAP P46, F2

Soieries du Mekong is the new Siem Reap gallery for the handwoven silk project based in remote Banteay Chhmar, which seeks to stem the tide of rural migration by creating employment opportunities in the village. Beautiful silk scarves and other delicate items are for sale. (www.soieriesdumekong. com; 688 Hup Guan St; ⊙10am-7pm)

Eric Raisina Couture House
FASHION & ACCESSORIES

124 🔒 MAP P42, E1

Renowned designer Eric Raisina brings a unique cocktail of influences to his couture. Born in Madagascar, raised in France and resident in Cambodia, he offers a striking collection of clothing and accessories. Ask him for a free tour of the workshop upstairs if he's around. There are additional branches around town, including at FCC Angkor. (📞063-963207; www.ericraisina.com; 75-81 Charles de Gaulle Blvd; ⊙store 8am-7pm, workshop 8-11am & 1-5pm)

Psar Chaa
MARKET

125 🔒 MAP P46, D6

When it comes to shopping in town, Psar Chaa is well stocked with anything you may want, and lots that you don't. Silverware, silk, wood carvings, stone carvings, Buddhas, paintings, rubbings, notes and coins, T-shirts, table

NIGEL PAVITT/GETTY IMAGES ©

mats...the list goes on. There are bargains to be had if you haggle patiently and humorously.

Bear in mind, however, that much of the souvenir items are imports from Thailand and China and not actually produced in Cambodia. Avoid buying old stone carvings that vendors claim are from Angkor. Whether or not they are real, buying these artefacts serves only to encourage their plunder and they will usually be confiscated by customs. (Old Market; ⊘6am-9pm)

Senteurs d'Angkor   ARTS & CRAFTS

126 🔒 MAP P46, E5

Opposite Psar Chaa, this shop has an eclectic collection of silk and carvings, as well as a superb range of traditional beauty products and spices, all made locally. The Kaya Spa is on-site. It targets rural poor and disadvantaged Cambodians for jobs and training, and sources local products from farmers.

Visit its Botanic Garden (p51) on Airport Rd, a sort of Willy Wonka's for the senses, where you can sample infused teas and speciality coffees. (☑063-964801; Pithnou St; ⊘7.30am-10.30pm)

Saomao   JEWELLERY

127 🔒 MAP P46, D5

A social enterprise selling wonderful silver and other jewellery, some made from bomb casings and brass bullets. Also has a wide variety of additional gifts, including coconut art, original *krama* and silks, pepper, and elegant runners and wall hangings. (☑012 818130; www.facebook.com/saomaoenterprise; St 9; ⊘8.30am-10pm Mon-Sat)

Rajana   ARTS & CRAFTS

128 🔒 MAP P46, C3

Sells quirky wooden and metalwork objects, well-designed silver and brass-bullet jewellery, and handmade cards. Rajana promotes fair-trade employment opportunities for Cambodians. (☑063-964744; www.rajanacrafts.org; Sivatha St; ⊘8am-11pm Mon-Sat)

Made in Cambodia   MARKET

King's Rd hosts the daily Made in Cambodia community market (see 73 ✖ Map p44, D6), bringing together many of the best local craftsfolk and creators in Siem Reap, many promoting good causes. (www.facebook.com/madeincambodiamarket; Siem Reap River Rd East; ⊘noon-10pm)

Smateria   FASHION & ACCESSORIES

129 🔒 MAP P46, C5

Recycling rocks here with funky bags made from construction nets, plastic bags, motorbike seat covers and more. It's a fair-trade enterprise employing some disabled Cambodians. (www.smateria.com; Alley West; ⊘10am-10pm)

Sra May
FASHION & ACCESSORIES

130 🔒 MAP P46, F2

Sra May is a social enterprise that uses traditional local materials such as palm leaves to create boxes and artworks. They also specialise in handwoven *krama*. This is also the drop-in office to book the PURE! Countryside Bicycle Tour (p33). (640 Hup Guan St; ⏲10am-6pm Mon-Sat)

Sirivan
FASHION & ACCESSORIES

131 🔒 MAP P46, F2

Established by French-Cambodian fashion designer Sirivan Chak Dumas, this shop has an elegant collection of women's and men's clothing in light linens and cottons, perfect for exploring the temples in high humidity. (www.sirivan.asia; 10 Hup Guan St; ⏲8am-7pm)

Louise Labatieres
HOMEWARES

132 🔒 MAP P46, F2

This little lifestyle boutique was the first to open on this strip and it still offers a treasure trove of designer homewares in silk, cotton, lacquer and ceramics. (www.louiselabatieres.com; 632 Hup Guan St; ⏲10am-7pm Mon-Sat)

Spicy Green Mango
FASHION & ACCESSORIES

133 🔒 MAP P46, C5

Small designer boutique with fun and funky fashion and accessories, in an old house that looks like it's straight out of Provence. (www.spicygreenmango.com; Alley West; ⏲10am-10pm)

Mooglee
CLOTHING

134 🔒 MAP P44, D6

Fun T-shirt shop with some original designs including elephants at Angkor, tigers at the temples and old Angkor travel posters. (www.mooglee.com; Wat Bo Rd; ⏲10am-10pm)

Bambou Indochine
CLOTHING

135 🔒 MAP P46, C5

Original clothing designs inspired by Indochina. A cut above the average souvenir T-shirts. (www.bambouindochine.com; Alley West; ⏲9am-10pm)

Garden of Desire
JEWELLERY

136 🔒 MAP P46, D5

High-end jewellery shop selling stunning modern pieces made with a mix of silver and stones mined in northeast Cambodia. Some works are modelled on sculptures from Banteay Srei and other temples. (www.gardenofdesire-asia.com; The Alley; ⏲10am-10pm)

Jayav Art
ART

137 🔒 MAP P42, E2

Inspired by all the beautiful Angkorian sculpture around the temples, but lacking the excess baggage space to carry replica statues all the way home? Talk to Jayav Art, which specialises in exquisite papier-mâché replica sculptures in various sizes. (☎089 787345; A25 Charles de Gaulle Blvd; ⏲7am-6pm)

Diwo Gallery ART

138 MAP P44, C8

Selling French photographer and writer Thierry Diwo's collection of art photography from around Angkor, as well as high-quality replica bronze, stone and wood sculptures. (www.tdiwo.com; Wat Svay District; ⏱9am-6pm)

McDermott Gallery ART

These are the famous sepia images you have seen of Angkor. Calendars, cards and striking images of the temples, plus regular exhibitions (see 60 ✪ Map p44, D3). (http://asiaphotos.net; FCC Angkor, Pokambor Ave; ⏱10am-10pm)

IKTT TEXTILES

139 MAP P44, B8

This traditional wooden house is home to the Japanese-run Institute for Khmer Traditional Textiles, which sells fine *krama* (checked scarves), throws and more. They also operate a homestay out at their silk farm in Angkor Thom District. (Institute for Khmer Traditional Textiles; www.iktt earth.org; Tonlé Sap Rd; ⏱9am-5pm)

T Galleria FASHION & ACCESSORIES

140 MAP P44, D1

Located next to the Angkor National Museum, this is a flagship DFS duty-free shop that stocks everything from Paul Smith to Prada. It is extremely popular with Chinese visitors who flock here for discounted luxury items, but prices aren't really low compared with discount outlets back home. (☏063-962511; www.dfs.com/en/siem-reap; 968 Charles de Gaulle Blvd; ⏱9am-10pm; 🛜)

Siem Reap Art Center MARKET

141 MAP P44, C6

One of the newer night markets in town, the Siem Reap Art Center has a range of handicrafts and souvenirs, and is connected to the Psar Chaa area via a traditional wooden bridge across the Siem Reap River. (South bank of Siem Reap River; ⏱8am-11pm)

House of Peace Association GALLERY

142 MAP P42, A2

The creation of leather *sbei tuoi* (shadow puppets) is a traditional Khmer art form, and the figures make a memorable souvenir. Characters include gods and demons from the *Reamker,* as well as exquisite elephants with intricate armour. The House of Peace Association, about 4km down NH6 on the way to the airport, makes and sells these puppets.

Small pieces start at US$15, while larger ones can be as much as US$150. (សមាគមផ្ទះសន្តិភាព; Airport Rd; ⏱9am-6pm)

Monument Books BOOKS

143 MAP P44, C6

Well-stocked bookstore near Psar Chaa, with an additional branch at the airport. (Pokambor Ave; ⏱9am-9pm)

Explore ◈
The Temples of Angkor

Welcome to heaven on earth. Angkor (អង្គរ) is the earthly representation of Mt Meru, the Mt Olympus of the Hindu faith and the abode of ancient gods. The temples are the perfect fusion of creative ambition and spiritual devotion. The Cambodian 'god-kings' of old each strove to better their ancestors in size, scale and symmetry, culminating in the world's largest religious building, Angkor Wat.

The temples of Angkor are a source of inspiration and national pride to all Khmers as they struggle to rebuild their lives after the years of terror and trauma. Today, the temples are a point of pilgrimage for all Cambodians, and no traveller to the region will want to miss their extravagant beauty. Angkor is one of the world's foremost ancient sites, with the epic proportions of the Great Wall of China, the detail and intricacy of the Taj Mahal, and the symbolism and symmetry of the Pyramids, all rolled into one.

Getting There & Around

The central temple area is just 8km from Siem Reap, and can be visited using anything from a car or motorcycle to a sturdy pair of walking shoes. For the ultimate Angkor experience, try a pick-and-mix approach, with a *moto, remork-moto* or car for one day to cover the remote sites, a bicycle to experience the central temples, and an exploration on foot for a spot of peace and serenity.

Neighbourhood Map on p80

Monks entering Bayon (p94) TYLER W. STIPP/SHUTTERSTOCK ©

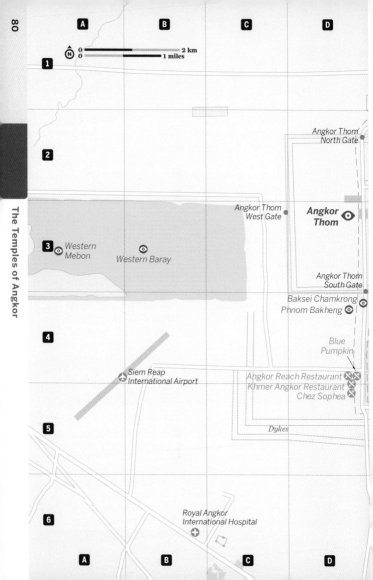

A **B** **C** **D**

N 0 ⎯⎯⎯⎯ 2 km
0 ⎯⎯⎯⎯ 1 miles

1

2

Angkor Thom
North Gate

Angkor Thom
West Gate

**Angkor
Thom**

3 Western
Mebon

Western Baray

Angkor Thom
South Gate

Baksei Chamkrong
Phnom Bakheng

Blue
Pumpkin

4

Siem Reap
International Airport

Angkor Reach Restaurant
Khmer Angkor Restaurant
Chez Sophea

5

Dykes

6

Royal Angkor
International Hospital

A **B** **C** **D**

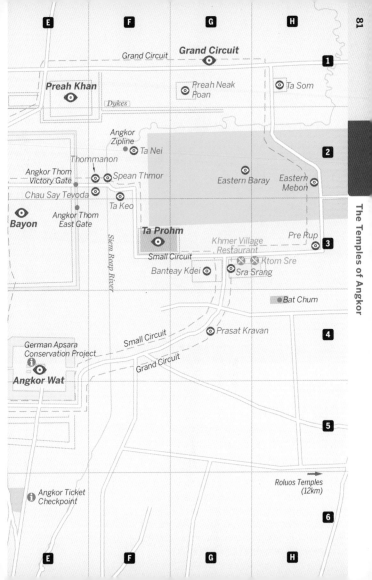

E **F** **G** **H**

Grand Circuit **Grand Circuit** 1

Preah Khan Preah Neak Poan Ta Som

Dykes

Angkor Zipline Ta Nei 2

Thommanon

Angkor Thom Victory Gate Spean Thmor Eastern Baray Eastern Mebon

Chau Say Tevoda

Ta Keo

Bayon Angkor Thom East Gate

Ta Prohm Pre Rup 3

Khmer Village Restaurant

Small Circuit Ktom Sre

Banteay Kdei Sra Srang

Siem Reap River

Bat Chum

Small Circuit Prasat Kravan 4

German Apsara Conservation Project

Grand Circuit

Angkor Wat

5

Roluos Temples (12km)

Angkor Ticket Checkpoint

6

E **F** **G** **H**

Top Sight
Angkor Wat

The traveller's first glimpse of Angkor Wat, the ultimate expression of Khmer genius, is matched by only a few select spots on earth. Built by Suryavarman II (r 1112–52) and surrounded by a vast moat, Angkor Wat is one of the most inspired monuments ever conceived by the human mind. Stretching around the central temple complex is an 800m-long series of bas-reliefs, and rising 55m above the ground is the central tower, which gives the whole ensemble its sublime unity.

◎ **MAP P80**

អង្គរវត្ត

incl in Angkor admission
1/3/7 days US$37/62/72

⏱5am-5.30pm

Symbol of a Nation

Angkor Wat is the heart and soul of Cambodia: it is the national symbol, the epicentre of Khmer civilisation and a source of fierce national pride. Since it was built, the temple has been in virtually continuous use and has never been abandoned to the elements. According to inscriptions, the construction of Angkor Wat involved 300,000 workers and 6000 elephants, yet was still not fully completed.

Simply unique, it is a stunning blend of spirituality and symmetry, an enduring example of humanity's devotion to its gods. Relish the very first approach, as that spine-tickling moment when you emerge on the inner causeway will rarely be felt again. It is the best-preserved temple at Angkor, and repeat visits are rewarded with previously unnoticed details.

While Suryavarman II may have planned Angkor Wat as his funerary temple or mausoleum, he was never buried and it is believed he may have died after returning from a failed expedition to subdue the Dai Viet (Vietnamese).

The Moat

Angkor Wat is surrounded by a 190m-wide moat, which forms a giant rectangle measuring 1.5km by 1.3km. From the west, a sandstone causeway crosses the moat. The sandstone blocks from which Angkor Wat was built were quarried more than 50km away (from the holy mountain of Phnom Kulen) and floated down the Siem Reap River on rafts. The logistics of such an operation are mind-blowing, consuming the labour of thousands – an unbelievable feat given the machinery we take for granted in contemporary construction projects.

Dedicated to Vishnu

The rectangular outer wall, which measures 1025m by 800m, has a gate on each side, but the main entrance, a 235m-wide porch richly

★ Top Tips

○ Allow at least two hours on-site for a visit to Angkor Wat; plan half a day if you want to decipher the bas-reliefs with a tour guide and ascend to Bakan.

○ Angkor Wat is very busy at sunrise so consider entering through the 'back door' that is the Eastern Causeway.

✗ Take a Break

There is an extensive selection of restaurants lined up opposite the entrance to Angkor Wat such as **Khmer Angkor Restaurant** (mains US$3-6; ⊘ 6am-6pm; 🛜) and **Angkor Reach Restaurant** (Map p80; mains US$3-6; ⊘ 6am-6pm; 🛜). There is also a handy branch of **Blue Pumpkin** (Map p80; www.bluepumpkin.asia; dishes US$2-8; ⊘ 7am-7pm; ❄ 🛜) turning out sandwiches, salads and ice creams. Pricier **Chez Sophea** (Map p80; 📞 012 858003; meals US$10-20; ⊘ 11am-10pm; 🛜) offers barbecued meat and fish.

decorated with carvings and sculptures, is on the western side. There is a statue of Vishnu, 3.25m in height and hewn from a single block of sandstone, located in the right-hand tower – this was originally housed in the central tower of the temple. Vishnu's eight arms hold a mace, a spear, a disc, a conch and other items. You may see locks of hair lying about. These are offerings both from young people preparing to get married and from pilgrims giving thanks for their good fortune.

An avenue, 475m long and 9.5m wide and lined with *naga* balustrades, leads from the main entrance to the central temple, passing between two graceful libraries (restored by a Japanese team) and then two pools, the northern one a popular spot from which to watch the sun rise.

Gallery of a Thousand Buddhas

The central temple complex consists of three storeys, each made of laterite, which enclose a square surrounded by intricately interlinked galleries. The Gallery of a Thousand Buddhas (Preah Poan) used to house hundreds of Buddha images before the war, but many of these were removed or stolen, leaving just the handful we see today.

Bakan Sanctuary

The corners of the second and third storeys are marked by towers, each topped with symbolic lotus-bud towers. The stairs to the upper level are immensely steep – because reaching the kingdom of the gods was no easy task. Also known as Bakan, the upper level of Angkor Wat was

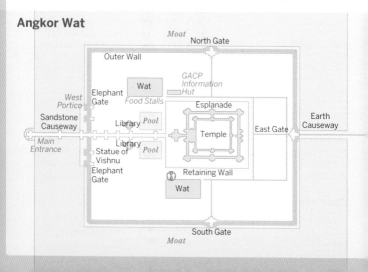

Angkor Wat

An Architectural Map of the Universe

There is much about Angkor Wat that is unique among the temples of Angkor. The most significant fact is that the temple is oriented towards the west. Symbolically, west is the direction of death, which once led many scholars to conclude that Angkor Wat must have existed primarily as a tomb. This idea was supported by the fact that the magnificent bas-reliefs of the temple were designed to be viewed in an anticlockwise direction, a practice that has precedents in ancient Hindu funerary rites. However, Vishnu is also frequently associated with the west, and it is now commonly accepted that Angkor Wat was originally dedicated to this Hindu deity.

Visitors to Angkor Wat are struck by its imposing grandeur and, at close quarters, its fascinating decorative flourishes and extensive bas-reliefs. Holy men at the time of Angkor must have revelled in its multilayered levels of meaning in much the same way a contemporary literary scholar might delight in James Joyce's *Ulysses*.

Eleanor Mannikka explains in her book *Angkor Wat: Time, Space and Kingship* that the spatial dimensions of Angkor Wat parallel the lengths of the four ages (Yuga) of classical Hindu thought. Thus the visitor to Angkor Wat who walks the causeway to the main entrance and through the courtyards to the final main tower, which once contained a statue of Vishnu, is metaphorically travelling back to the first age of the creation of the universe.

Like the other temple-mountains of Angkor, Angkor Wat also replicates the spatial universe in miniature. The central tower is Mt Meru, with its surrounding smaller peaks, bounded in turn by continents (the lower courtyards) and the oceans (the moat). The seven-headed *naga* becomes a symbolic rainbow bridge for humanity to reach the abode of the gods.

closed to visitors for several years, but it is once again open (8am to 5pm daily, except religious holidays) to a limited number per day with a timed queuing system. This means it is possible to complete the pilgrimage with an ascent to the 55m summit: savour the cooling breeze, take in the extensive views and then find a quiet corner in which to contemplate the symmetry and symbolism of this Everest of temples. Clothing that covers to the elbows and knees is required to visit this upper level of Angkor Wat.

Bas-Reliefs

Stretching around the outside of the central temple complex is an 800m-long series of intricate and astonishing bas-reliefs. The majority were completed in the 12th century, but in the 16th century several new reliefs were added to unfinished panels.

The bas-reliefs were once sheltered by the cloister's wooden roof, which long ago rotted away except for one original beam in the western half of the north gallery. The other roofed sections are reconstructions.

The Battle of Kurukshetra

The southern portion of the west gallery depicts a battle scene from the Hindu *Mahabharata* epic, in which the Kauravas (coming from the north) and the Pandavas (coming from the south) advance upon each other, meeting in furious battle. Infantry are shown on the lowest tier, with officers on elephants, and chiefs on the second and third tiers.

Some of the more interesting details include (from left to right): a dead chief lying on a pile of arrows, surrounded by his grieving parents and troops; a warrior on an elephant who, by putting down his weapon, has accepted defeat; and a mortally wounded officer, falling from his carriage into the arms of his soldiers. Over the centuries, some sections have been polished (by the millions of hands that fall upon them) to look like black marble. The portico at the southwestern corner is decorated with sculptures representing characters from the *Ramayana*.

The Army of Suryavarman II

The remarkable western section of the south gallery depicts a triumphal battle march of Suryavarman II's army. In the southwestern corner about 2m from the floor is Suryavarman II on an elephant, wearing the royal tiara and armed with a battle-axe; he is shaded by 15 parasols and fanned by legions of servants.

Angkor Wat Central Structure

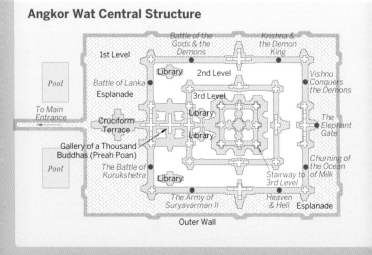

Compare this image of the king and with the image of Rama in the northern gallery and you'll notice an uncanny likeness that helped reinforce the aura of the god-king.

Further on is a procession of well-armed soldiers and officers on horseback; among them are bold and warlike chiefs on elephants. Just before the end of this panel is the rather disorderly Siamese mercenary army, with their long headdresses and ragged marching, at that time allied with the Khmers in their conflict with the Chams. The Khmer troops have square breastplates and are armed with spears; the Thais wear skirts and carry tridents.

The rectangular holes seen in the Army of Suryavarman II relief were created when, long ago, pieces of the scene containing inscriptions (reputed to possess magical powers) were removed.

Heaven & Hell

The eastern half of the south gallery depicts the punishments and rewards of the 37 heavens and 32 hells. On the left, the upper and middle tiers show fine gentlemen and ladies proceeding towards 18-armed Yama (the judge of the dead) seated on a bull; below him are his assistants, Dharma and Sitragupta. On the lower tier, devils drag the wicked along the road to hell.

To Yama's right, the tableau is divided into two parts by a horizontal line of *garuda* (mythical half-man, half-bird crea-

Apsaras

Angkor Wat is famous for its beguiling *apsaras* (heavenly nymphs). Almost 2000 *apsaras* are carved into the walls of Angkor Wat, each of them unique, and there are 37 different hairstyles for budding stylists to check out. Many of these exquisite *apsaras* have been damaged by centuries of bat droppings and urine, but they are now being restored by the **German Apsara Conservation Project** (GACP; Map p80; www.gacp-angkor.de; ⏱7am-5pm). The organisation operates a small information booth in the northwestern corner of Angkor Wat, near the modern wat, where beautiful B&W postcards and images of Angkor are available.

ture): above, the elect dwell in beautiful mansions, served by women and attendants; below, the condemned suffer horrible tortures that might have inspired the Khmer Rouge. The ceiling in this section was restored by the French in the 1930s.

Churning of the Ocean of Milk

The southern section of the east gallery is decorated by the most famous of the bas-relief scenes at Angkor Wat, the Churning of the Ocean of Milk. This brilliantly executed carving depicts 88 *asuras* on the left, and 92 *devas*, with crested helmets, churning up the sea to extract from it the elixir of immortality.

The demons hold the head of the serpent Vasuki and the gods hold its tail. At the centre of the sea, Vasuki is coiled around Mt Mandala, which turns and churns up the water in the tug of war between the demons and the gods. Vishnu, incarnated as a huge turtle, lends his shell to serve as the base and pivot of Mt Mandala. Brahma, Shiva, Hanuman (the monkey god) and Lakshmi (the goddess of wealth and prosperity) all make appearances, while overhead a host of heavenly female spirits sing and dance in encouragement. Luckily for us, the gods won through, as the *apsaras* above were too much for the hot-blooded devils to take. Restoration work by the World Monuments Fund was completed on this incredible panel in 2012.

The Elephant Gate
This **gate**, which has no stairway, was used by the king and others for mounting and dismounting elephants directly from the gallery. North of the gate is a Khmer inscription recording the erection of a nearby stupa in the 18th century.

Vishnu Conquers the Demons
The northern section of the east gallery shows a furious and desperate encounter between Vishnu, riding on a *garuda*, and innumerable devils. Needless to say, he slays all comers. This gallery was most likely completed in the 16th century, and the later carving is notably inferior to the original work from the 12th century.

Krishna & the Demon King
The eastern section of the north gallery shows Vishnu incarnated

Apsara carvings

Top Kings of Angkor

A mind-numbing array of kings ruled the Khmer empire from the 9th century AD to the 14th century. All of their names include the word 'varman', which means 'armour' or 'protector'. Forget the small fry and focus on the big fish:

Jayavarman II (r 802–50) Founder of the Khmer empire in AD 802.

Indravarman I (r 877–89) Builder of the first baray (reservoir), and of Preah Ko and Bakong.

Yasovarman I (r 889–910) Moved the capital to Angkor and built Lolei and Phnom Bakheng.

Jayavarman IV (r 928–42) Usurper king who moved the capital to Koh Ker.

Rajendravarman II (r 944–68) Builder of Eastern Mebon, Pre Rup and Phimeanakas.

Jayavarman V (r 968–1001) Oversaw construction of Ta Keo and Banteay Srei.

Suryavarman I (r 1002-49) Expanded the empire into much of Laos and Thailand.

Udayadityavarman II (r 1049–65) Builder of the pyramidal Baphuon and the Western Mebon.

Suryavarman II (r 1112–52) Legendary builder of Angkor Wat and Beng Mealea.

Jayavarman VII (r 1181–1219) The king of the god-kings, building Angkor Thom, Preah Khan and Ta Prohm.

as Krishna riding a *garuda*. He confronts a burning walled city, the residence of Bana, the demon king. The *garuda* puts out the fire and Bana is captured. In the final scene Krishna kneels before Shiva and asks that Bana's life be spared.

Battle of the Gods & the Demons

The western section of the north gallery depicts the battle between the 21 gods of the Brahmanic pantheon and various demons. The gods are featured with their traditional attributes and mounts. Vishnu has four arms and is seated on a *garuda*, while Shiva rides a sacred goose.

Battle of Lanka

The northern half of the west gallery shows scenes from the *Ramayana*. In the Battle of Lanka, Rama (on the shoulders of Hanuman), along with his army of monkeys, battles 10-headed, 20-armed

Ravana, captor of Rama's beautiful wife Sita. Ravana rides a chariot drawn by monsters and commands an army of giants.

Getting There

Angkor Wat is at the heart of the Angkor Archaeological Park, 6km north of Siem Reap. Transport options from Siem Reap include *moto*, *remork-moto* and car. Cycling is another easy option; the road here is flat and straight.

Nearby: Phnom Bakheng

Located around 400m south of Angkor Thom, the main attraction at **Phnom Bakheng** (ភ្នំបាខែង; incl in Angkor admission 1/3/7 days US$37/62/72; ☉5am-7pm) is the sunset view over Angkor Wat. For many years, the whole affair turned into a circus, with crowds of tourists ascending the slopes of the hill and jockeying for space. Today numbers are restricted to just 300 visitors at any one time, so get here early (4pm) to guarantee a sunset spot. The temple, built by Yasovarman I (r 889–910), has five tiers, with seven levels.

Phnom Bakheng also lays claim to being home to the first of the temple-mountains built in the vicinity of Angkor. Yasovarman I chose Phnom Bakheng over the Roluos area, where the earlier capital (and temple-mountains) had been located.

At the base are – or were – 44 towers. Each of the five tiers had 12 towers. The summit of the temple has four towers at the cardinal

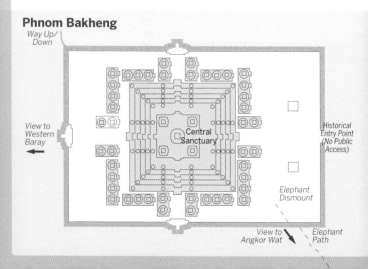

Phnom Bakheng

Way Up/Down

View to Western Baray ←

Central Sanctuary

Historical Entry Point (No Public Access)

Elephant Dismount

View to Angkor Wat ↘ *Elephant Path*

points of the compass as well as a central sanctuary. All of these numbers are of symbolic significance. The seven levels represent the seven Hindu heavens, while the total number of towers, excluding the central sanctuary, is 108, a particularly auspicious number and one that correlates to the lunar calendar.

Some prefer to visit in the early morning, when it's cool (and crowds are light), to climb the hill. That said, the sunset over the Western Baray is very impressive from here. Allow about two hours for the sunset experience.

Nearby: Baksei Chamkrong

Located southwest of the south gate of Angkor Thom, **Baksei Chamkrong** (បក្សីចាំក្រុង; Map p80; ☉7.30am-5.30pm) is one of the few brick edifices in the immediate vicinity of Angkor. A well-proportioned though petite temple, it was once decorated with a covering of lime mortar. Like virtually all of the structures of Angkor, it opens to the east. In the early 10th century, Harshavarman I erected five statues in this temple: two of Shiva, one of Vishnu and two of Devi.

Nearby: Western Baray & Western Mebon

The **Western Baray** (បារាយណ៍ទឹកថ្លា; Map p80; ☉7.30am-5.30pm), measuring an incredible 8km by 2.3km, was excavated by hand to provide water for the intensive cultivation of lands around Angkor. These enormous *barays* (reservoirs) weren't dug out, but were huge dykes built up around the edges. In the centre of the Western Baray is the ruin of the Western Mebon temple, where the giant bronze statue of Vishnu, now in the National Museum in Phnom Penh, was found. The Western Mebon is accessible by boat.

The Western Baray is the main local swimming pool around Siem Reap. There is a small beach of sorts at the western extreme, complete with picnic huts and inner tubes for rent, which attracts plenty of Khmers at weekends.

Top Sight

Angkor Thom & Bayon

It's hard to imagine any building bigger or more beautiful than Angkor Wat, but in Angkor Thom (Great City) the sum of its parts add up to a greater whole. Set over 10 sq km, the aptly named last great capital of the Khmer empire took monumental to a whole new level. In the centre of the walled enclosure are the city's most important monuments, including Bayon, Baphuon, Phimeanakas and the Terrace of Elephants.

Angkor Thom is 8km from Siem Reap. Transport options from Siem Reap include bicycle, *moto*, *remork-moto* and car. If coming from Angkor Wat, you'll enter Angkor Thom through the South Gate, just 2km away.

Angkor Thom

Centred on Bayon, the surreal state temple of Jayavarman VII, Angkor Thom (Map p80) is enclosed by a formidable *jayagiri* (square wall), 8m high and 12km long, and encircled by a 100m-wide *jayasindhu* (moat) that would have stopped all but the hardiest invaders in their tracks. This architectural layout is an expression of Mt Meru surrounded by the oceans.

Siem Reap River, the river that runs from the foothills of Phnom Kulen to Tonlé Sap lake, was diverted to run through most of the major temples and *barays* of Angkor, including Angkor Thom's vast moat.

If arriving at Angkor Thom from Angkor Wat, you'll enter through the south gate. From Ta Prohm, you'll enter through the Victory Gate on the eastern side. The immense **north gate** (pictured left) of Angkor Thom connects the walled city with Preah Khan and the temples of the Grand Circuit. The west gate leads to the Western Baray.

The Gates of Angkor Thom

It is the gates that grab you first, flanked by a vast representation of the Churning of the Ocean of Milk, 54 demons and 54 gods engaged in an epic tug of war on the causeway. Each gate towers above the visitor, the magnanimous faces of the Bodhisattva Avalokiteshvara staring out over the kingdom. Imagine being a peasant in the 13th century approaching the forbidding capital for the first time. It would have been an awe-inspiring yet unsettling experience to enter such a gateway and come face to face with the divine power of the god-kings.

The **south gate** is most popular, as it has been fully restored and many of the heads (mostly copies) remain in place. The gate is on the main road into Angkor Thom from Angkor Wat, and it gets very busy. More peaceful are the **east** and **west** gates, found at the end of

★ Top Tips

○ Head to Angkor Thom's east gate for a *Tomb Raider* photo opportunity; this is the only gate that doesn't have a road passing through it.

○ Watch out for the macaques that hang around the forest between the south gate and Bayon. They have been known to grab food or drinks and even bite.

○ Set aside half a day for an in-depth exploration of Angkor Thom.

✕ Take a Break

There are food stalls near the Terrace of the Leper King and Preah Palilay that serve up Cambodian classics, plus more stalls in front of Preah Pithu, where there are also bathrooms. Ice cream vans are also parked in this area.

dirt trails. The east gate was used as a location in *Tomb Raider*. The causeway at the west gate has completely collapsed, leaving a jumble of ancient stones sticking out of the soil.

Bayon

At the heart of Angkor Thom is the 12th-century **Bayon** (បាយ័ន; ⏱7.30am-5.30pm), the mesmerising, if slightly mind-bending, state temple of Jayavarman VII. It epitomises the creative genius and inflated ego of Cambodia's most celebrated king. Its 54 Gothic towers are famously decorated with 216 gargantuan smiling faces of Avalokiteshvara, which bear more than a passing resemblance to the great king himself.

Some say that the Khmer empire was divided into 54 provinces at the time of Bayon's construction, hence the 54 pairs of all-seeing eyes keeping watch on the kingdom's outlying subjects.

The Face Temple

Unique, even among its cherished contemporaries, the temple's architectural audacity was a definitive political statement about the change from Hinduism to Mahayana Buddhism. Known as the 'face temple' thanks to its iconic visages, these huge heads glare down from every angle, exuding power and control with a hint of humanity. This was precisely the blend required to hold sway over such a vast empire, ensuring the disparate and far-flung population yielded to Jayavarman VII's magnanimous will. As you walk around, a dozen or more of the heads are visible at any one time, full face or in profile, sometimes level with your eyes, sometimes staring down from on high.

Mysterious Origins

Though Bayon is now known to have been built by Jayavarman VII, for many years its origins were unknown. Shrouded in dense jungle, it also took researchers some time to realise that it stands in the exact centre of the city of Angkor Thom. There is still much mystery associated with Bayon – including its exact function and symbolism – and this seems only appropriate for a monument whose signature is an enigmatic smiling face.

Unlike Angkor Wat, which looks impressive from all angles, Bayon looks rather like a glorified pile of rubble from a distance. It's only when you enter the temple and make your way up to the third level that its magic becomes apparent.

Spirit Levels

The basic structure of Bayon comprises a simple three levels, which correspond more or less to three distinct phases of building. This is because Jayavarman VII began construction of this temple at an advanced age, so he was never confident it would be completed. Each time one phase was completed, he moved on to the next. The first two levels are square and adorned with bas-reliefs. They lead up to a third, circular level, with the towers and their faces.

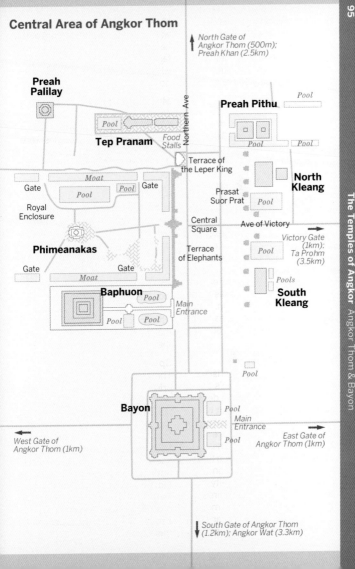

Central Area of Angkor Thom

North Gate of
Angkor Thom (500m);
Preah Khan (2.5km)

Preah Palilay

Pool

Preah Pithu

Pool

Pool

Northern Ave

Pool

Pool

Food
Stalls

Tep Pranam

Terrace of
the Leper King

North Kleang

Gate

Moat

Pool

Pool

Gate

Royal
Enclosure

Prasat
Suor Prat

Pool

Ave of Victory

Central
Square

Phimeanakas

Victory Gate
(1km);
Ta Prohm
(3.5km)

Gate

Gate

Terrace
of Elephants

Pool

Moat

South Kleang

Baphuon

Pool

Pools

Pool

Pool

Pool

Main
Entrance

Terrace
of Elephants

Pool

Bayon

Pool

Main
Entrance

West Gate of
Angkor Thom (1km)

Pool

East Gate of
Angkor Thom (1km)

South Gate of Angkor Thom
(1.2km); Angkor Wat (3.3km)

The Temples of Angkor Angkor Thom & Bayon

Bayon Bas-Reliefs

The famous carvings on the outer wall of the first level show vivid scenes of everyday life in 12th-century Cambodia. The bas-reliefs on the second level don't have the epic proportions of those on the first level and tend to be fragmented.

Chams on the Run

Moving in a clockwise direction from just south of the east gate you'll encounter your first bas-relief, Chams on the Run, a three-level panorama. On the first tier, Khmer soldiers march off to battle – check out the elephants and the ox-carts, which are almost exactly like those still used in Cambodia today. The second tier depicts coffins being carried back from the battlefield. In the centre of the third tier, Jayavarman VII, shaded by parasols, is shown on horseback followed by legions of concubines (to the left).

Hindus Praying to a Linga

The first panel north of the southeastern corner shows Hindus praying to a *linga* (phallic symbol). This image was probably originally a Buddha, later modified by a Hindu king.

Naval Battle

The Naval Battle panel has some of the best-carved reliefs. The scenes depict a naval battle between the Khmers and the Chams (the latter with head coverings), and everyday life around Tonlé Sap lake, where the battle was fought. Look for images of people picking lice from each other's hair, of hunters and, towards the western end of the panel, a woman giving birth.

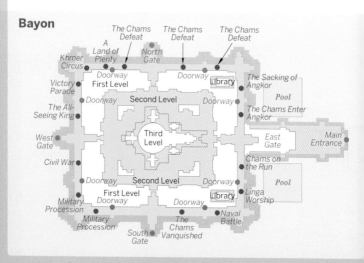

Bayon

Chams Vanquished

In the Chams Vanquished bas-relief, scenes from daily life are featured while the battle between the Khmers and the Chams takes place on the shore of Tonlé Sap lake, where the Chams are soundly thrashed. Scenes include two people playing chess, a cockfight and women selling fish in the market. The scenes of meals being prepared and served are in celebration of the Khmer victory.

Military Procession

The most western relief of the south gallery, depicting a military procession, is unfinished, as is the panel showing elephants being led down from the mountains and Brahmans being chased up two trees by tigers.

Civil War

The next panel depicts scenes that some scholars maintain is a civil war. Groups of people, some of them armed, confront each other; the violence escalates until elephants and warriors join the melee.

All-Seeing King

Just north of the civil war panel, the fighting continues on a smaller scale in the All-Seeing King. Here an antelope is being swallowed by a gargantuan fish; among the smaller fish is a prawn, under which an inscription proclaims that the king will seek out those in hiding.

Celebration of his Victory

The next panel depicts a procession that includes the king

An Ancient Megacity

Angkor Thom was built in part as a reaction to the surprise sacking of Angkor by the Chams, after Jayavarman VII (r 1181–1219) decided that his empire would never again be vulnerable at home. At the city's height, it may have supported a population of one million people in the surrounding region.

(carrying a bow). Presumably it is a celebration of his victory.

Khmer Circus

At the western corner of the northern wall is a Cambodian circus. A strongman holds three dwarfs, and a man on his back is spinning a wheel with his feet; above is a group of tightrope walkers. To the right of the circus, the royal court watches from a terrace, below which is a procession of animals. Some of the reliefs in this section remain unfinished.

A Land of Plenty

On the northern side of the temple, this bas-relief shows two rivers – one next to the doorpost and the other a few metres to the right – teeming with fish.

Chams Defeated

On the lowest level of the unfinished three-tiered Chams Defeated, the Cham armies are being defeated and expelled from the Khmer kingdom. The next panel depicts the Cham armies advancing, and the badly deteriorated third panel shows the Chams (on the left) chasing the Khmers.

The Sacking of Angkor

Featuring the war of 1177, the sacking of Angkor depicts the Khmers defeated by the Chams. The wounded Khmer king is being lowered from the back of an elephant and a wounded Khmer general is being carried on a hammock suspended from a pole. Directly above, despairing Khmers are getting drunk. The Chams (on the right) are in hot pursuit of their vanquished enemy.

Chams Enter Angkor

The next panel, the Chams Enter Angkor, depicts a meeting of the Khmer and Cham armies. Notice the flag bearers among the Cham troops (on the right). The Chams were defeated in the war, which ended in 1181, as depicted on the first panel in the sequence.

Baphuon

Some have called **Baphuon** (បាពួន; ⏲7.30am-5.30pm) the 'world's largest jigsaw puzzle'. Before the civil war the Baphuon was painstakingly taken apart piece-by-piece by a team of archaeologists, but their meticulous records were destroyed during the Khmer Rouge regime, leaving experts with 300,000 stones to put back into place. After years of excruciating research, this temple has been partially restored.

It takes around one hour to fully explore Baphuon, or less if you skip the upper levels.

Layout

In its heyday, Baphuon would have been one of the most spectacular of Angkor's temples. Located 200m northwest of Bayon, it's a pyramidal representation of mythical Mt Meru. Construction probably began under Suryavarman I and was later completed by Udayadityavarman II. It marked the centre of the capital that existed before the construction of Angkor Thom.

Reclining Buddha

Baphuon is approached by a 200m elevated walkway made of sandstone. Clamber under the walkway for an incredible view of the hundreds of pillars supporting it. In the 16th century, the retaining wall on the western side of the second level was fashioned into a 60m reclining Buddha. The central structure is 43m high.

Terrace of the Leper King

The **Terrace of the Leper King** (ព្រះលានស្ដេចគម្លង់; ⏲7.30am-5.30pm) is just north of the Terrace of Elephants. Dating from the late 12th century, it is a 7m-high platform, on top of which stands a nude, though sexless, statue. The front retaining walls of the terrace are decorated with at least five tiers of meticulously executed carvings. On the southern side of the Terrace of the Leper King, there is access to a hidden terrace with exquisitely preserved carvings.

A Royal Crematorium

The nude statue here is yet another of Angkor's mysteries, and various theories have been advanced to

The Cast of Characters Around Angkor

The temples of Angkor are intricately carved with myths and legends, symbols and signs, and a cast of characters in their thousands. Deciphering them can be quite a challenge, so here we've highlighted some of the most commonly seen around the temples. For more help unravelling the carvings of Angkor, pick up a copy of *Images of the Gods* by Vittorio Reveda.

Apsaras Heavenly nymphs or goddesses, also known as *devadas;* these beautiful female forms decorate the walls of many temples.

Asuras These devils feature extensively in representations of the Churning of the Ocean of Milk, such as at Angkor Wat.

Devas The 'good gods' in the creation myth of the Churning of the Ocean of Milk.

Garuda Vehicle of Vishnu; this half-man, half-bird creature features in some temples and was combined with his old enemy the *nagas* to promote religious unity under Jayavarman VII.

Kala The temple guardian appointed by Shiva; he had such an appetite that he devoured his own body and appears only as a giant head above doorways. Also known as Rehu.

Makara A giant sea serpent with a reticulated jaw; features on the corner of pediments, spewing forth a *naga* or some other creature.

Naga The multi-headed serpent, half-brother and enemy of *garudas*. Controls the rains and, therefore, the prosperity of the kingdom; seen on causeways, doorways and roofs. The seven-headed *naga*, a feature at many temples, represents the rainbow, which acts as a bridge between heaven and earth.

Nandi The mount of Shiva; there are several statues of Nandi dotted about the temples, although many have been damaged or stolen by looters.

Rishi A Hindu wise man or ascetic, also known as *essai;* these bearded characters are often seen sitting cross-legged at the base of pillars or flanking walls.

Yama God of death who presides over the underworld and passes judgement on whether people continue to heaven or hell.

explain its meaning. Legend has it that at least two of the Angkor kings had leprosy, and the statue may represent one of them. Another theory – a more likely explanation – is that the statue is of

Yama, the god of death, and that the Terrace of the Leper King housed the royal crematorium. The original statue is held at Phnom Penh's National Museum.

The carved walls include seated *apsaras* and kings wearing pointed diadems, armed with short double-edged swords and accompanied by the court and princesses, the latter adorned with beautiful rows of pearls.

A Hidden Terrace

On the southern side of the Terrace of the Leper King (facing the Terrace of Elephants), there is access to the front wall of a hidden terrace that was covered up when the outer structure was built, a sort of terrace within a terrace. The four tiers of *apsaras* and other figures, including *nagas*, look as fresh as if they had been carved yesterday, thanks to being covered up for centuries. Some of the figures carry fearsome expressions. As you follow the inner wall of the Terrace of the Leper King, notice the increasingly rough chisel marks on the figures, an indication that this wall was never completed, like many of the temples at Angkor.

Terrace of Elephants

The 350m-long **Terrace of Elephants** (ទីលានជល់ដំរី; ⏱7.30am-5pm) was used as a giant viewing stand for public ceremonies and served as a base for the king's grand audience hall. Try to imagine the pomp and grandeur of the Khmer empire at its height, with infantry, cavalry, horse-drawn chariots and elephants parading across the Central Square in a colourful procession, pennants and standards aloft. Looking on is the god-king, shaded by multi-tiered parasols and attended by mandarins and handmaidens bearing gold and silver utensils.

The Terrace of Elephants has five piers extending towards the Central Square – three in the centre and one at each end. The middle section of the retaining wall is decorated with life-size *garudas* and lions; towards either end are the two parts of the famous parade of elephants, complete with their Khmer mahouts.

Preah Palilay

Preah Palilay (ព្រះបាលិលៃ្យ; ⏱7.30am-5.30pm) is located about 200m north of the Royal Enclosure's northern wall. It was erected during the rule of Jayavarman VII and originally housed a Buddha, which has long since vanished. There are several huge tree roots looming large over the central tower making for a memorable photo opportunity of a classic 'jungle temple'.

Phimeanakas & the Royal Palace

Phimeanakas (ភិមានអាកាស; ⏱7.30am-5pm) stands close to the centre of a walled area that once housed the royal palace. There's very little left of the palace today except for two sandstone pools near the northern wall. Phimeanakas means 'Celestial Palace', and some scholars say that it was once topped by a golden spire. Phimeanakas is currently undergoing restoration and the upper level is off-limits to visitors.

Construction of the palace began under Rajendravarman II, although it was used by Jayavarman V and Udayadityavarman I. It was later added to and embellished by Jayavarman VII and his successors. The Royal Enclosure is fronted to the east by the Terrace of Elephants. The northwestern wall of the Royal Enclosure is very atmospheric, with immense trees and jungle vines cloaking the outer side, easily visible on a forest walk from Preah Palilay to Phimeanakas.

The temple is another pyramidal representation of Mt Meru, with three levels. Most of the decorative features are broken or have disappeared.

Preah Pithu

Located across Northern Ave from Tep Pranam, **Preah Pithu** (ព្រះពិធូ; ⏱7.30am-5.30pm) is a group of 12th-century Hindu and Buddhist temples enclosed by a wall. It includes some beautifully decorated terraces and guardian animals in the form of elephants and lions. It sees few tourists, so it's a good place to explore at a leisurely pace, taking in the impressive jungle backdrop.

The Kleangs & Prasat Suor Prat

Along the eastern side of the Central Square are two groups of buildings, called **Kleangs** (ប្រាសាទឃ្លាំង និងប្រាសាទសួរប្រ័ត្រ; ⏱7.30am-

5pm). The North Kleang and the South Kleang may at one time have been palaces. The North Kleang has been dated from the period of Jayavarman V. Along the Central Square, in front of the two Kleangs, are 12 laterite towers – 10 in a row and two more at right angles facing the Ave of Victory – known as the Prasat Suor Prat, meaning 'Temple of the Tightrope Dancers'.

Archaeologists believe the towers, which form an honour guard along Central Square, were constructed by Jayavarman VII. It is likely that each one originally contained either a *linga* or a statue. It is said artists performed for the king on tightropes or rope bridges strung between these towers, hence the name.

According to 13th-century Chinese emissary Chou Ta-Kuan, the towers of Prasat Suor Prat were also used for public trials of sorts. During a dispute the two parties would be made to sit inside two towers, one party eventually succumbing to illness and proven guilty.

Tep Pranam

An 82m by 34m cruciform Buddhist terrace, 150m east of Preah Palilay, **Tep Pranam** (ទេពប្រណម្យ; ⏱7.30am-5.30pm) was once the base of a pagoda of lightweight construction. The nearby 4.5m-high Buddha is a reconstruction of the original. A group of Buddhist nuns lives in a wooden structure close by.

Walking Tour 🚶

Angkor Thom

The great walled city of Angkor Thom is a manageable size, contains some of the most spectacular temples found in the region and is blanketed in mature forest, offering plenty of shade. Following back trails into this mighty temple complex is the perfect way to escape the crowds and to enjoy some of the lesser-known temples.

Walk Facts

Start South gate of Angkor Thom

Finish Bayon, Angkor Thom

Length 7km; four to five hours

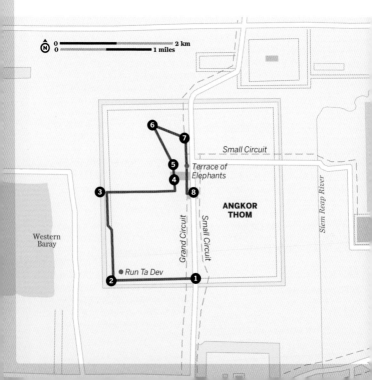

❶ South Gate

Starting out at the spectacular **Angkor Thom south gate** (p93), admire the immense representation of the Churning of the Ocean of Milk, where 54 demons and 54 gods flank the bridge to the walled city. Ascend the wall and head west to enjoy views of the vast moat to the left and the thick jungle to the right.

❷ Prasat Chrung

Reaching the southwest corner, admire **Prasat Chrung**, one of four identical temples marking the corners of the city. Head down below to see the water outlet of Run Ta Dev; this once-powerful city was criss-crossed by canals in its heyday.

❸ West Gate

Back on the gargantuan wall, continue to the **west gate** (p93), looking out for a view to the immense Western Baray on your left. Descend to admire the artistry of the four faces of Avalokiteshvara, the Buddha of Compassion. Wander east along the path into the heart of Angkor Thom, but don't be diverted by the beauty of Bayon, as this is best saved until last.

❹ Baphuon

Veer north into **Baphuon** (p98) and wander to the back of what was built as the state temple of Udayadityavarman II in the mid-11th century.

❺ Royal Enclosure & Phimeanakas

Pass the small temple of **Phimeanakas** (p100) and the former royal palace compound, an area of towering trees, tumbling walls and atmospheric foliage.

❻ Preah Palilay

Continue further north to petite but pretty **Preah Palilay** (p100), overshadowed by an impressive cluster of kapok trees. Several huge tree roots loom large over the central tower.

❼ Terrace of the Leper King

Make for the mainstream with a walk through the **Terrace of the Leper King** (p98) and along the front of the royal viewing gallery, the Terrace of Elephants. If there's time, zigzag east to visit the later-ite towers of Prasat Suor Prat and the atmospheric Buddhist temple of Preah Pithu.

❽ Bayon

Otherwise, continue to the top billing of **Bayon** (p94): weird yet wonderful, this is one of the most enigmatic of the temples at Angkor. Take your time to decipher the bas-reliefs before venturing up to the legendary faces of the upper level.

Top Sight

Ta Prohm & the Temples of the Small Circuit

Ta Prohm, the 'Tomb Raider temple', is cloaked in dappled shadow, its crumbling towers and walls locked in the slow muscular embrace of vast root systems. Undoubtedly the most atmospheric ruin at Angkor, Ta Prohm should be high on the hit list of every visitor. The so-called Small Circuit includes a whole host of temples near Ta Prohm, including Ta Nei, Ta Keo and Sra Srang.

The temples of the Small Circuit lie between 8km and 12km from Siem Reap and are accessible by *moto/remork-moto*/car for about US$10/15/30. It is also possible to explore by bicycle.

Ta Prohm

The lure of **Ta Prohm** (តាព្រហ្ម; Map p80; incl in Angkor admission 1/3/7 days US$37/62/72; ⏰7.30am-5.30pm) lies in the fact that, unlike the other monuments of Angkor, it has been swallowed by the jungle, and looks very much the way most of the monuments of Angkor appeared when European explorers first stumbled upon them. Well, that's the theory. In fact, the jungle is pegged back and only the largest trees are left in place, making it manicured rather than raw like Beng Mealea. Still, a visit to Ta Prohm is an otherworldly experience. There is a poetic cycle to this venerable ruin, with humanity first conquering nature to rapidly create, and nature once again conquering humanity to slowly destroy. If Angkor Wat is testimony to the genius of the ancient Khmers, Ta Prohm reminds us equally of the awesome fecundity and power of the jungle.

The temple is at its most impressive early in the day. Allow as much as two hours to visit, especially if you want to explore the maze-like corridors and iconic tree roots.

Monastery of the King

Built from 1186 and originally known as Rajavihara (Monastery of the King), Ta Prohm was a Buddhist temple dedicated to the mother of Jayavarman VII. It is one of the few temples in the Angkor region where an inscription provides information about the temple's dependents and inhabitants.

Ta Prohm is a temple of towers, closed courtyards and narrow corridors. Many of the corridors are impassable, clogged with jumbled piles of delicately carved stone blocks dislodged by the roots of long-decayed trees. Bas-reliefs on bulging walls are carpeted with lichen, moss and creeping plants, and shrubs sprout from the roofs of monumental porches. Trees, hundreds of years old, tower overhead, their leaves filtering the sunlight and casting a greenish pall over the whole scene.

★ Top Tips

○ Plan to arrive at Ta Prohm before 7.30am to be among the first to explore the temple. Entering via the remote north gate is a good way to leave the crowds behind.

○ Look out for a small jungle path between Chau Say Tevoda and the Victory Gate of Angkor Thom. Follow it and the path eventually emerges at the east gate, forgotten in the jungle.

✕ Take a Break

Some lively local restaurants overlook Sra Srang and these make a great lunch or drink stop. **Ktom Sre** (Map p80; ☏078 334496; Sra Srang; mains US$3-8; ⏰6am-6pm) offers a signature coconut roast chicken in banana leaf. **Khmer Village Restaurant** (Map p80; ☏012 390583; http://khmervillagerestaurant.com; Sra Srang; mains US$4-8; ⏰6am-5pm) has a huge menu of Cambodian, Chinese, Thai and international dishes.

According to an inscription stele from Ta Prohm, close to 80,000 people were required to maintain or attend the temple, among them more than 2700 officials and 615 dancers.

Tomb Raider at Ta Prohm

The most popular of the many strangulating root formations is that on the inside of the easternmost *gopura* (entrance pavilion) of the central enclosure, nicknamed the Crocodile Tree. Another is the '*Tomb Raider* tree' where a scene from the Angelina Jolie movie was shot back in 2000. It used to be possible to climb onto the damaged galleries, but this is now prohibited, to protect both temple and visitor. Many of these precariously balanced stones weigh a tonne or more and would do some serious damage if they came down. Ta Prohm is currently under stabilisation and restoration by an Indian team of archaeologists working with their Cambodian counterparts.

Banteay Kdei

An immense Buddhist monastery from the latter part of the 12th century, **Banteay Kdei** (បន្ទាយក្ដី; Map p80; ⊙7.30am-5.30pm) is surrounded by four concentric walls. Each of its four entrances is decorated with *garudas*, which hold aloft one of Jayavarman VII's favourite themes: the four faces of Avalokiteshvara.

The outer wall of Banteay Kdei measures 500m by 700m. The southeast wall of Ta Prohm and the northwest wall of Banteay Kdei are just 10m apart. The inside of the central tower was never finished and much of the temple is in a ruinous state due to hasty construction. It is considerably

Ta Prohm

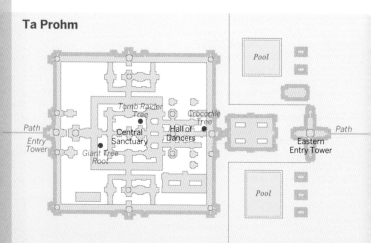

On Location with Tomb Raider

Several sequences for the film *Lara Croft: Tomb Raider* (2001), starring Angelina Jolie as Lara Croft, were shot around the temples of Angkor. The Cambodia shoot opened at Phnom Bakheng, with Lara looking through binoculars for the mysterious temple. The baddies were already trying to break in through the east gate of Angkor Thom by pulling down a giant (polystyrene!) *apsara*. Reunited with her custom Land Rover, Lara made a few laps around Bayon before discovering a back way into the temple from Ta Prohm. After battling a living statue and dodging Daniel Craig (aka 007) by diving off the waterfall at Phnom Kulen, she emerged in a floating market in front of Angkor Wat, as you do. She came ashore here before borrowing a mobile phone from a local monk and venturing into the Gallery of a Thousand Buddhas, where she was healed by the abbot.

less busy than nearby Ta Prohm, however, and this alone can justify a visit. Allow about one hour to visit Banteay Kdei and admire the view over nearby Sra Srang.

Sra Srang

East of Banteay Kdei is a vast pool of water, **Sra Srang** (ស្រះស្រង់; Pool of Ablutions; Map p80; incl in Angkor admission 1/3/7 days US$37/62/72; ☺5am-5.30pm), measuring 800m by 400m, which was reserved as a bathing pool for the king and his consorts.

A tiny island in the middle of Sra Srang once bore a wooden temple, of which only the stone base remains. This is a beautiful body of water from which to take in a quiet sunrise.

Ta Keo

A stark, undecorated temple, **Ta Keo** (តាកែវ; Map p80; incl in Angkor admission 1/3/7 days US$37/62/72; ☺7.30am-5.30pm) would have undoubtedly been one of the finest of Angkor's structures had it been finished. Built by Jayavarman V, it was dedicated to Shiva and was the first Angkorian monument built entirely of sandstone. The summit of the central tower, which is surrounded by four lower towers, is almost 50m high. The four towers at the corners of a square and a fifth tower in the centre are typical of many Angkorian temple-mountains.

No one is certain why work was never completed, but a likely cause may have been the death of Jayavarman V. Others contend that the hard sandstone was impossible to carve and that explains the lack of decoration. According to inscriptions, Ta Keo was struck by lightning during construction, which may have been seen as a bad omen and led to its abandonment. Allow about 30 minutes to visit Ta Keo.

Ta Nei

There is something of the spirit of Ta Prohm at **Ta Nei** (តានី; Map p80; incl in Angkor admission 1/3/7 days

US$37/62/72; ⊙7.30am-5.30pm), albeit on a lesser scale, with moss and tentacle-like roots covering many outer areas of this small temple. However, the number of visitors is also on a lesser scale, making it very atmospheric. Ta Nei was built by Jayavarman VII (r 1181–1219).

It can be accessed via a jungle road from Ta Keo (located 800m north) through the forest, a guaranteed way to find solitude. Including the access, allow about one hour to visit Ta Nei.

Chau Say Tevoda

Just east of Angkor Thom's Victory Gate is **Chau Say Tevoda** (ចៅសាយទេវតា; Map p80; ⊙7.30am-5.30pm). It was probably built during the second quarter of the 12th century, under the reign of Suryavarman II, and dedicated to Shiva and

Vishnu. It has been renovated by the Chinese to bring it up to the condition of its twin temple, Thommanon.

Thommanon

Although unique, **Thommanon** (ធម្មនន្ទ; Map p80; incl in Angkor admission 1/3/7 days US$37/62/72; ⊙7.30am-5.30pm) complements its neighbour Chau Say Tevoda, as it was built to a similar design around the same time and was dedicated to Shiva and Vishnu. It is in good condition thanks to extensive work undertaken by the EFEO (École française d'Extrême-Orient) in the 1960s.

Spean Thmor

Located 200m east of Thommanon, **Spean Thmor** (ស្ពានថ្ម, Stone Bridge; Map p80) is the only large bridge remaining in the immediate vicinity

Chau Say Tevoda

Guide to the Guides

Countless books on Angkor have been written over the years, with more and more new titles coming out, reflecting Angkor's rebirth as the world's top cultural hotspot. Here are just a few of the best:

A Guide to the Angkor Monuments (Maurice Glaize) The definitive 1944 guide, downloadable for free at www.theangkorguide.com.

A Passage Through Angkor (Mark Standen) One of the best photographic records of the temples.

A Pilgrimage to Angkor (Pierre Loti) One of the most beautifully written books on Angkor, based on the author's 1910 journey.

Ancient Angkor (Claude Jacques) Written by one of the foremost scholars on Angkor, this is a very readable guide to the temples, with photos by Michael Freeman.

Angkor: An Introduction to the Temples (Dawn Rooney) Probably the most popular contemporary guide.

Angkor – Heart of an Asian Empire (Bruno Dagens) The story of the 'discovery' of Angkor, complete with lavish illustrations.

Angkor: Millennium of Glory (various authors) A fascinating introduction to the history, culture, sculpture and religion of the Angkorian period.

Khmer Heritage in the Old Siamese Provinces of Cambodia (Etienne Aymonier) Aymonier journeyed through Cambodia in 1901 and visited many of the major temples.

The Angkor Guide (Andrew Booth; www.angkorguidebook.com) Excellent guide to the temples of Angkor with input from leading academics, beautiful overlay illustrations and profits helping to fund local education.

The Customs of Cambodia (Chou Ta-Kuan) The only eyewitness account of Angkor, by a Chinese emissary who spent a year at the Khmer capital in the late 13th century.

of Angkor with an arch and several piers. It vividly highlights how the water level has changed course over the centuries and may offer clues to the collapse of Angkor's extensive irrigation system.

Jayavarman VII constructed many roads with immense stone bridges spanning watercourses.

There are more spectacular examples of these ancient bridges elsewhere in Siem Reap Province, such as Spean Preah Tuos, with 19 arches, in Kompong Kdei on NH6 from Phnom Penh; and Spean Ta Ong, a 77m bridge with a beautiful *naga*, forgotten in the forest about 28km east of Beng Mealea.

Top Sight

Preah Khan & the Temples of the Grand Circuit

The temple of Preah Khan is one of the largest complexes at Angkor, a maze of vaulted corridors, fine carvings and lichen-clad stonework. It is a good counterpoint to Ta Prohm and generally sees slightly fewer visitors. Other temples in the so-called Grand Circuit include the water temple of Preah Neak Poan, Ta Som, Eastern Mebon and the royal crematorium of Pre Rup.

The temples of the Grand Circuit lie between 11km and 15km from Siem Reap and are accessible by *moto* (US$10), *remork-moto* (US$10) and car (US$30). It is also possible to explore by bicycle on a 30km-ride.

Preah Khan

Built by Jayavarman VII, **Preah Khan** (ព្រះខ័ន;
Sacred Sword; Map p80; incl in Angkor admission
1/3/7 days US$37/62/72; ⏱7.30am-5.30pm) prob-
ably served as his temporary residence while
Angkor Thom was being built. The central sanctuary of the temple was dedicated in AD 1191.

Preah Khan is a genuine fusion temple, with
the eastern entrance dedicated to Mahayana
Buddhism with equal sized doors, and the
other cardinal directions dedicated to Shiva,
Vishnu and Brahma with successively smaller
doors, emphasising the unequal nature of
Hinduism.

A large stone stela tells us much about Preah
Khan's role as a centre for worship and learn-
ing. Originally located within the first eastern
enclosure, this stela is now housed safely at
Angkor Conservation (p31). The temple was
dedicated to 515 divinities, and during the
course of a year, 18 major festivals took place
here, requiring a team of thousands just to
maintain the place.

Preah Khan is in a reasonable state of preservation thanks to the ongoing restoration efforts
of the **World Monuments Fund** (WMF; www.
wmf.org).

A Vast Temple

Preah Khan covers a very large area, but the
temple itself is within a rectangular enclosing
wall of around 700m by 800m. Four proces-
sional walkways approach the gates of the
temple, and these are bordered by another
stunning depiction of the Churning of the
Ocean of Milk, as in the approach to Angkor
Thom, although most of the heads have
disappeared. From the central sanctuary, four
long, vaulted galleries extend in the cardinal
directions. Many of the interior walls of Preah
Khan were once coated with plaster that was
held in place by holes in the stone. Today many

★ **Top Tips**

○ Look out for the
incredible *garudas*
mounted on the
outer walls of Preah
Khan temple: you
can sponsor one for
US$50,000 to assist
the World Monument
Fund in their restora-
tion work.

○ When heading to
the eastern side of
Preah Khan, look out
for the marker stones
that line the walkway.
Originally all these
niches contained
Buddha images, but
were removed by
Hindu militants.

○ Pre Rup gets
crowed at sunset, so
consider an alterna-
tive such as Eastern
Mebon, which offers
impressive views
over the rice fields.

🍴 **Take a Break**

There are plenty of
food and drink stalls
dotted about. The
best spot for a break
is the eastern exit of
Preah Khan, where
there is a viewpoint
over the Jayatataka
Baray. This is where
the Angkor kings
of old would have
boarded the royal
barge to visit Preah
Neak Poan.

delicate reliefs remain, including *rishi* and *apsara* carvings.

A Grecian Exile?

The main entrance to Preah Khan is in the east, but most tourists enter at the west gate near the main road and walk the length of the temple to the east gate before doubling back to the central sanctuary and exiting at the north gate. Approaching from the west, there is little clue to nature's genius, but on the outer retaining wall of the east gate is a pair of trees with monstrous roots embracing, one still reaching for the sky. There is also a curious Grecian-style two-storey structure in the temple grounds, the purpose of which is unknown, but it looks like an exile from Athens. Another option is to enter from the north and exit from the east.

Ta Som

Located to the east of Preah Neak Poan, **Ta Som** (តាសោម; Map p80; incl in Angkor admission 1/3/7 days US$37/62/72; ☉7.30am-5.30pm) is one of the late-12th-century Buddhist temples of prolific builder Jayavarman VII. The most impressive feature here is the huge tree completely overwhelming the eastern *gopura*, providing one of the most popular photo opportunities in the Angkor area.

Eastern Mebon & Eastern Baray

The Hindu temple of **Eastern Mebon** (មេបុណ្យខាងកើត; Map p80; ☉7.30am-5.30pm), erected by Rajendravarman II, would have once been situated on an islet in the centre of

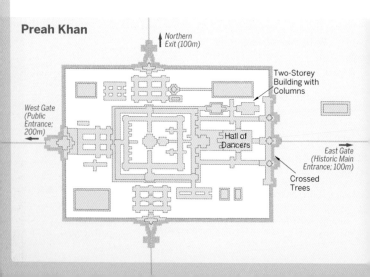

Preah Khan

↑ Northern Exit (100m)

Two-Storey Building with Columns

West Gate (Public Entrance; 200m)

Hall of Dancers

East Gate (Historic Main Entrance; 100m) →

Crossed Trees

the enormous Eastern Baray, but it is now very much on dry land. Its temple-mountain form is topped off by a quintet of towers. The elaborate brick shrines are dotted with neatly arranged holes, which attached the original plasterwork. The base of the temple is guarded at its corners by perfectly carved stone figures of elephants. The Eastern Mebon is flanked by earthen ramps, a clue that this temple was never finished and a good visual guide to how the temples were constructed.

The enormous one-time reservoir known as the **Eastern Baray** (បារាយណ៍ខាងកើត; Map p80) was excavated by Yasovarman I, who marked its four corners with stelae. This basin, now entirely dried up, was the most important of the public works of Yasodharapura, Yasovarman I's capital, and is 7km by 1.8km. It was originally fed by the Siem Reap River.

Pre Rup

Built by Rajendravarman II, **Pre Rup** (ប្រែរូប; Map p80; ⏱5am-7pm) is about 1km south of the Eastern Mebon. The temple consists of a pyramid-shaped temple-mountain with the uppermost of the three tiers carrying five lotus towers.

The brick sanctuaries here were once decorated with a plaster coating, fragments of which remain on the southwestern tower; there are some amazingly detailed lintel carvings here. Several of the outermost eastern towers are perilously

Preah Khan (p111)

close to collapse and are propped up by an army of wooden supports.

Pre Rup means 'Turning the Body' and refers to a traditional method of cremation in which a corpse's outline is traced in the cinders: this suggests that the temple may have served as an early royal crematorium.

The temple is one of the most popular sunset spots around Angkor, as the view over the surrounding rice fields of the Eastern Baray is beautiful, although some lofty trees have rather obscured it these days.

Preah Neak Poan

The Buddhist temple of **Preah Neak Poan** (នាគព័ន្ធ, Temple of the Intertwined Nagas; Map p80;

incl in Angkor admission 1/3/7 days US$37/62/72; ⊙7.30am-5.30pm) is a petite yet perfect creation constructed by Jayavarman VII in the late 12th century. It has a large square pool surrounded by four smaller square pools. In the middle of the central pool is a circular 'island' encircled by the two *nagas* whose intertwined tails give the temple its name.

It's a safe bet that if an 'Encore Angkor' casino is eventually developed in Las Vegas or Macau, Preah Neak Poan will provide the blueprint for the ultimate swimming complex.

The Legend of Avalokiteshvara
In the pool around the central island there were once four statues, but only one remains, reconstructed from the debris by the French archaeologists who cleared the site.

The curious figure has the body of a horse supported by a tangle of human legs. It relates to a legend that Avalokiteshvara once saved a group of shipwrecked followers from an island of ghouls by transforming into a flying horse. A beautiful replica of this statue decorates the main roundabout at Siem Reap International Airport.

Water Features
Water once flowed from the central pool into the four peripheral pools via ornamental spouts, which can still be seen in the pavilions at each axis of the pool. The spouts are in the form of an elephant's head, a horse's head, a lion's head and a human head. The pool was used for ritual purification rites.

Preah Neak Poan was once in the centre of a huge 3km-by-900m

Preah Neak Poan

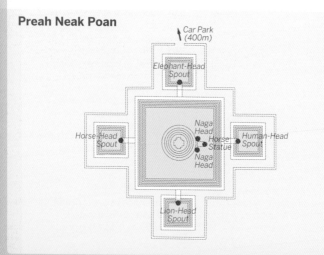

baray serving Preah Khan, known as Jayataka, once again partially filled with water due to a new opening in the dyke road. Access is restricted to the edge of the complex via a wooden causeway, so a visit takes only 30 minutes.

Prasat Kravan

Uninspiring from the outside, the interior brick carvings concealed within its towers are the hidden treasure of **Prasat Kravan** (ប្រាសាទក្រវ៉ាន់; Map p80; ⏲ 7.30am-5.30pm). The five brick towers, arranged in a north–south line and oriented to the east, were built for Hindu worship in AD 921. The structure is unusual in that it was not constructed by royalty; this accounts for its slightly distant location (just south of the road between Angkor Wat and Banteay Kdei), away from the other temples.

Prasat Kravan was partially restored in 1968, returning the brick carvings to their former glory. The images of Vishnu in the largest central tower show the eight-armed deity on the back wall, taking the three gigantic steps with which he reclaimed the world on the left wall, and riding a *garuda* on the right wall. The northern-most tower displays bas-reliefs of Vishnu's consort, Lakshmi.

The Long Strider

One of Vishnu's best-loved incarnations was when he appeared as the dwarf Vamana, and proceeded to reclaim the world from the evil demon king Bali. The dwarf politely asked the demon king for a comfortable patch of ground upon which to meditate, saying that the patch need only be big enough so that he could easily walk across it in three paces. The demon agreed, only to see the dwarf swell into a mighty giant who strode across the universe in three enormous steps. From this legend, depicted at Prasat Kravan, Vishnu is sometimes known as the 'long strider'.

Top Sight
Banteay Srei District

Famous for its petite pink-coloured temple, there is more to Banteay Srei than its iconic Angkor sites, such as the 'River of a Thousand Lingas' at Kbal Spean and the 12th-century temple of Banteay Samré. New destinations and experiences, including homestays, village walks, ox-cart rides, fruit farms and handicraft workshops, are under development to encourage visitors to stay longer and explore further.

Popular destinations in Banteay Srei lie between 15km and 50km from Siem Reap and are best accessed by car or *remork-moto*. Expect to pay a surcharge due to the long distances involved.

Banteay Srei

Considered by many to be the jewel in the crown of Angkorian art, **Banteay Srei** (បន្ទាយស្រី; incl in Angkor admission 1/3/7 days US$37/62/72; ⏰7.30am-5.30pm) is cut from stone of a pinkish hue and includes some of the finest stone carving anywhere on earth. Begun in AD 967, it is one of the smallest sites at Angkor, but what it lacks in size it makes up for in stature. Banteay Srei, a Hindu temple dedicated to Shiva, is wonderfully well preserved and many of its carvings are three-dimensional.

Dating the Art Gallery of Angkor

Banteay Srei, the art gallery of Angkor, was initially assumed to date from the 13th or 14th centuries, as it was thought that the refined carving must have come at the end of the Angkor period. It was later dated to AD 967, from inscriptions found at the site.

Built by a Brahman

Banteay Srei is one of the few temples around Angkor to be commissioned not by a king but by a brahman, who may have been a tutor to Jayavarman V. The temple is square and has entrances at the east and west, with the east approached by a causeway. Of interest are the lavishly decorated libraries and the three central towers, which are decorated with male and female divinities and beautiful filigree relief work. Banteay Srei means 'Citadel of the Women', and it is said that it must have been built by a woman, as the elaborate carvings are supposedly too fine for the hand of a man.

Scenes from the Ramayana

Classic carvings at Banteay Srei include delicate women with lotus flowers in hand and traditional skirts clearly visible, as well as breathtaking recreations of scenes from the *Ramayana* adorning the library pediments (carved inlays above a lintel). However, the sum of the parts is no greater than the whole –

★ Top Tips

⊙ From Siem Reap, Banteay Samré, Banteay Srei and Kbal Spean can be combined in a day trip by *remork-moto* (US$25–30) or car (US$60).

⊙ Arrive at Banteay Srei when it opens to avoid the crowds.

⊙ It takes 45 minutes to explore Banteay Srei temple, but allow 1½ hours to visit the information centre and explore the area.

⊙ Carry plenty of water when climbing up to Kbal Spean; there is none available beyond the parking area.

⊙ Visit www.visit banteaysrei.com for more on community-based tourism in the Banteay Srei District.

✕ Take a Break

There are several restaurants near Banteay Srei, Banteay Samré and Kbal Spean. Preah Dak village is renowned for its **Naom Banchok Noodle Stalls** (Preah Dak; noodles 4000r; ⏰6am-6pm), which hug the main road to Banteay Srei.

almost every inch of these interior buildings is covered in decoration. Standing watch over such perfect creations are the mythical guardians, all of which are copies of originals stored in the National Museum.

A Test Case for Restoration

Banteay Srei was the first major temple restoration undertaken by the EFEO in 1930 using the anastylosis method. The project, as evidenced today, was a major success and soon led to other larger projects such as the restoration of Bayon. Banteay Srei is also the first to have been given a full makeover in terms of facilities, with a large car park, a designated dining and shopping area, clear visitor information and a state-of-the-art exhibition on the history of the temple and its restoration.

Nearby: Kbal Spean

A spectacularly carved riverbed, **Kbal Spean** (ក្បាលស្ពាន, River of a Thousand Lingas; incl in Angkor admission 1/3/7 days US$37/62/72; ⏱7.30am-5.30pm) is set deep in the jungle to the northeast of Angkor. More commonly referred to in English as the 'River of a Thousand Lingas', the name actually means 'bridgehead', a reference to the natural rock bridge here. *Lingas* (phallic symbols) have been elaborately carved into the riverbed, and images of Hindu deities are dotted about the area.

Kbal Spean was 'discovered' in 1969, but the area was soon off-limits due to the civil war, only becoming safe again in 1998. At no point during a visit to Kbal Spean should you leave well-trodden paths, as there may be landmines in the area.

Banteay Srei

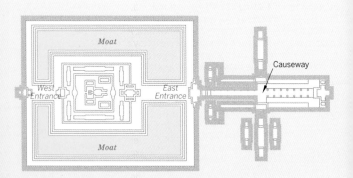

Angkor Centre for Conservation of Biodiversity

Conveniently located at the base of the trail to Kbal Spean is the **Angkor Centre for Conservation of Biodiversity** (ACCB, មជ្ឈមណ្ឌលអង្គរសម្រាប់ការអភិរក្សជីវចម្រុះ; ☏099 604017; www.accb-cambodia.org; donation US$3; ⏰tours 9am & 1pm'Mon-Sat; 🚻), which is committed to rescuing, rehabilitating and releasing threatened wildlife into the Cambodian forests. It also operates conservation breeding programs for selected threatened species in an attempt to preserve them from extinction. Daily tours (in English) are available at 9am and 1pm (except Sunday), taking about 1½ hours.

The centre takes care of about 45 species totalling more than 550 animals. It is possible to see pileated gibbon, Indochinese silvered langur, several turtle and tortoise species, green peafowl, small carnivores and a variety of birds of prey. There are also several large wading birds, including the impressive sarus crane and one of the largest collections of threatened storks in the world.

A minimum donation of US$3 per person is requested. Tours outside core hours and special private tours are available upon request at variable costs. It is recommended to book tours in advance by phone or email. Note that you don't need an Angkor pass to visit ACCB, only to visit Kbal Spean.

Hindu Deities

It is a 2km uphill walk to the carvings, along a pretty path that winds its way up into the jungle, passing by some interesting boulder formations along the way. The path eventually splits to the waterfall or the river carvings. It is best to start with the river carvings and work back down to the waterfall to cool off. There is an impressive carving of Vishnu on the upper section of the river, followed by a series of carvings at the bridgehead itself, some of which were hacked off in the past few years, but have since been replaced by excellent replicas. This area is now roped off to protect the carvings from further damage.

A Thousand Lingas

Following the river down, there are several more impressive carvings of Vishnu, and Shiva with his consort Uma, and further downstream hundreds of *lingas* appear on the riverbed. At the top of the waterfall are many animal images, including a cow and a frog, and a path winds around the boulders to a wooden staircase leading down to the base of the falls. Between January and June visitors will be disappointed to see very little water here. The best time to visit is between July and December.

The excellent **Borey Sovann Restaurant** (meals US$3-6; ⏰11am-6pm; 📶), located near the entrance to Kbal Spean, is a great

Butterfly at the Banteay Srey Butterfly Centre

tion has resulted in some looting during the past few decades. The area consists of a central temple with four wings, preceded by a hall and also accompanied by two libraries, the southern one remarkably well preserved.

The whole ensemble is enclosed by two large concentric walls around what would have been the unique feature of an inner moat, now dry.

Banteay Samré is 400m east of the Eastern Baray. A visit here can be combined with a trip to Banteay Srei and/or Phnom Bok.

Nearby: Cambodia Landmine Museum

Established by DIY de-miner Aki Ra, this **museum** (សារមន្ទីរគ្រាប់មីនកម្ពុជា និងមូលនិធិសង្គ្រោះ; www.cambodialandminemuseum.org; US$5; ⏰7.30am-5pm) has eye-opening displays on the curse of landmines in Cambodia. The collection includes mines, mortars, guns and weaponry, and there is a mock minefield where visitors can attempt to locate the deactivated mines. Proceeds from the museum are ploughed into mine-awareness campaigns. The museum is about 25km from Siem Reap, near Banteay Srei.

place to wind down before or after an ascent to the River of a Thousand Lingas.

From the car park, the visit takes about two hours including the walk, nearer three hours with a natural shower or a picnic. Last entry to Kbal Spean is at 3.30pm, so plan ahead. A day trip here can be combined with Angkor Centre for Conservation of Biodiversity, Banteay Srei and the Cambodia Landmine Museum.

Nearby: Banteay Samré

Banteay Samré (បន្ទាយសំរែ; ⏰7.30am-5.30pm) dates from the same period as Angkor Wat and was built by Suryavarman II. The temple is in a fairly healthy state of preservation due to some extensive renovation work, although its isola-

Nearby: Banteay Srey Butterfly Centre

The **Banteay Srei Butterfly Centre** (ស្ងួនមេអំបៅបន្ទាយស្រី; www.angkorbutterfly.com; adult/child US$5/2; ⏰9am-5pm) is one of the largest fully enclosed butterfly centres in Southeast Asia, with more than 30 species of Cambodian butterflies fluttering about. It is a good experience for children, as they can see the whole life cycle from egg to caterpillar to cocoon to butterfly.

The centre aims to provide a sustainable living for the rural poor and most of the butterflies are farmed around Phnom Kulen. It's about 7km before Banteay Srei temple on the left side of the road.

Nearby: Phnom Bok

One of three temple-mountains built by Yasovarman I in the late 9th or early 10th century, peaceful but remote **Phnom Bok** (ភ្នំបូក; ⏰7.30am-5.30pm), which is about 25km from Siem Reap, sees few visitors. The small temple is in reasonable shape, but it is the views of Phnom Kulen to the north and the plains of Angkor to the south from this 212m hill that make it worth the trip.

The remains of a 5m linga are visible at the opposite end of the hill and it's believed there were similar linga at Phnom Bakheng and Phnom Krom.

There is a long, winding trail snaking up the hill at Phnom Bok, which takes about 20 minutes to climb, plus a faster cement staircase, but the latter is fairly exposed. Avoid the heat in the middle of the day and carry plenty of water, which can be purchased locally.

Phnom Bok is clearly visible from the road to Banteay Srei. It is accessed by continuing east on the road to Banteay Samré for another 6km. It is possible to loop back to Siem Reap via the temples of Roluos by heading south instead of west on the return journey, and gain some rewarding glimpses of the countryside. Unfortunately, it is not a sensible place for sunrise or sunset, as it would require a long journey in the dark.

Nearby: Chau Srei Vibol

This petite hilltop **temple** (ចៅស្រីវិបុល; ⏰7.30am-5.30pm) is actually part of a larger complex that spanned the entire hill. It is relatively under-visited compared with more centrally located temples, making it an atmospheric option for sunset. The central sanctuary is in a ruined state but is nicely complemented by the construction of an early 20th-century wat nearby.

Surrounding the base of the hill are laterite walls, each with a small entrance hall in reasonable condition, outlining the dimensions of what was once a significant temple. To get here, turn east off the Bakong to Anlong Veng highway at a point about 8km north of NH6, or 5km south of Phnom Bok. There is a small sign (easy to miss) that marks the turn. Locals are friendly and helpful should you find yourself lost.

Top Sight
Phnom Kulen

Considered by Khmers to be the most sacred mountain in Cambodia, Phnom Kulen is a popular place of pilgrimage on weekends and during festivals. It played a significant role in the history of the Khmer empire, as it was from here in AD 802 that Jayavarman II proclaimed himself a devaraja (god-king), giving birth to the Cambodian kingdom. From 1970 until as late as 1998, it was a stronghold of the Khmer Rouge.

ភ្នំគូលែន

www.adfkulen.org

US$20

🕑 6-11am to ascend, noon-5pm to descend

Home of the Gods

For Indian Hindus, the Himalayas represent Mt Meru, the home of the gods, while the Khmer kings of old adopted Phnom Kulen as their symbolic Mt Meru. A beautiful road winds its way through some spectacular jungle scenery, emerging on the plateau after a 12km ascent. The road eventually splits: the left fork leads to the picnic spot, waterfall and ruins of a 9th-century temple; the right fork continues over a bridge (you'll find the riverbed carvings around here) to the base of Wat Preah Ang Thom, which sits at the summit of the mountain and houses the large reclining Buddha carved into the sandstone boulder upon which it is built. This is the focal point of a pilgrimage for Khmer people, so it is important to take off your shoes and any head covering before climbing the stairs to the sanctuary. These days the views from the 487m peak are partially obstructed by foliage run amok.

Tomb Raider Waterfall

The waterfall is an attractive spot and was featured in *Lara Croft: Tomb Raider*. However, it could be much more beautiful were it not for all the litter left here by families picnicking at the weekend. Near the top of the waterfall is a jungle-clad temple known as Prasat Krau Romeas, dating from the 9th century.

There are plenty of other Angkorian sites on Phnom Kulen, including as many as 20 minor temples around the plateau, the most important of which is Prasat Rong Chen, the first pyramid or temple-mountain to be constructed in the Angkor area.

Sra Damrei & Bat Cave

Most impressive of all are the giant stone animals or guardians of the mountain, known as Sra Damrei (Elephant Pond). These are quite difficult to reach, particularly during the wet season. The few people who make it are rewarded with a life-

★ Top Tips

○ It is only possible to go up Phnom Kulen before 11am and only possible to come down after midday, to avoid vehicles meeting on the narrow road.

○ Never leave well-trodden paths, as there may be landmines in some remote areas.

○ Speak to Mr Sean (012 827728), head of the Phnom Kulen Motorbike Taxi Association, about arranging transport to explore the more remote sites on Phnom Kulen.

✕ Take a Break

Small restaurants and food stalls are around the parking area at the base of Wat Preah Ang Thom. More atmospheric are the picnic restaurants located by the river about the waterfall. Pay around 10,000r to rent a pavilion, and order the food from surrounding vendors, including barbecued chicken, pork and fish and various local fruits.

size replica of a stone elephant and smaller statues of lions, a frog and a cow. These were constructed on the southern face of the mountain and from here there are spectacular views across the plains below.

About 1km below Sra Damrei is the so-called Bat Cave, a large cave that is home to ancient shrines and a colony of bats. Getting to Sra Damrei and the Bat Cave requires taking a *moto* from Wat Preah Ang Thom for about 12km on very rough trails – don't try to find it on your own. Expect to pay the *moto* driver about US$10 for a two-hour trip to explore this area.

Longer Day Trips

Other impressive sites that can be included in an adventurous day trip around Phnom Kulen include the ancient rock carvings of Poeung Tbal, an atmospheric site of enormous boulders, and the partially restored temple of Damrei Krap. Add these to the mix and it will cost more like US$15 to explore on the back of a motorbike for three hours or more.

The Lost City of Mahendraparvata

Phnom Kulen hit the headlines in 2013 thanks to the 'discovery' of a lost city known as Mahendraparvata in Angkorian times. Using jungle-piercing LIDAR (Light Detection and Ranging) radar technology, the structures of a more extensive archaeological site have been unveiled beneath the jungle canopy. However, it wasn't quite as dramatic a discovery as initially reported, as Phnom

Kulen had long been known as an important archaeological site. However, the LIDAR research confirmed the size and scale of the ancient city, complete with canals and *baray*, in the same way NASA satellite imagery had helped identify the size and scale of the greater Angkor hydraulic water system more than a decade earlier. Some new temples and features were identified beneath the jungle, but remain remote and inaccessible due to the terrain and the possibility of landmines.

The Archaeology and Development Foundation (ADF; www.adfkulen.org) has been working to excavate the vestiges of Mahendraparvata since 2008.

Getting There

Phnom Kulen is a huge plateau around 50km from Siem Reap and about 15km from Banteay Srei. To get here on the toll road, take the well-signposted right fork just before Banteay Srei village and go straight ahead at the crossroads. Just before the road starts to climb the mountain, there is a barrier and it is here that the admisson charge is levied.

Moto drivers are likely to want about US$20 or more to bring you out here, and rented cars will hit passengers with a surcharge, more than double the going rate for Angkor; forget coming by *remork-moto* as the hill climb is just too tough. With the long journey here, it is best to plan on spending the best part of a day exploring, although it can be combined with either Banteay Srei or Beng Mealea.

Phnom Kulen waterfall (p123)

Top Sight
Koh Ker

Once inaccessible and abandoned to the forests of the north, Koh Ker (pronounced ko-kayer) was the capital of the Angkorian empire from AD 928 to AD 944. According to inscriptions, in ancient times the city was known as Lingapura (City of Lingams) or Chok Gargyar (possibly City at a Glance). The principal monument is Mayan-looking Prasat Thom, a 55m-wide, 40m-high sandstone-faced pyramid whose seven tiers offer spectacular views across the forest.

កោះកេរ្ដិ៍
US$10
🕑7.30am-5.30pm

Prasat Thom

The largest monument at Koh Ker is **Prasat Thom** (Prasat Kompeng; ⏱7.30am-5.30pm). The staircase to the top is open to a limited number of visitors and the views are spectacular if you can stomach the heights. Some 40 inscriptions, dating from 932 to 1010, have been found here.

Prasat Krahom

The second-largest structure at Koh Ker, **Prasat Krahom** (Red Temple; ⏱7.30am-5.30pm) (Red Temple) is so named for the red bricks from which it is constructed. Sadly, none of the carved lions for which this temple was once known remain, though there's still plenty to see, with stone archways and galleries leaning hither and thither. A *naga*-flanked causeway and a series of sanctuaries, libraries and gates lead past trees and vegetation-covered ponds. Just west of Prasat Krahom, at the far western end of a half-fallen colonnade, are the remains (most of the head) of a statue of Nandi.

South of this central group is a 1185m-by-548m *baray* known as the **Rahal**. It is fed by the Sen River, which supplied water to irrigate the land in this arid area.

Prasat Leung & Prasat Bram

Some of the largest Shiva *linga* in Cambodia can still be seen in four temples about 1km northeast of Prasat Thom, collectively known as **Prasat Leung** (⏱7.30am-5.30pm). The largest is found in Prasat Thneng, while Prasat Balang is similarly well endowed.

Among the many other temples that are found around Koh Ker, **Prasat Bram** (⏱7.30am-5.30pm) is a real highlight. It consists of a collection of brick towers, at least two of which have been completely smothered by voracious

★ **Top Tips**

• Most visitors combine a visit to Beng Mealea (p130) and Koh Ker in a long day trip.

• Many of the Koh Ker temples were mined during the war, but most have now been cleared. Do not stray from trodden paths or wander into the forest, as there may be landmines within a few hundred metres of the temples.

• To really appreciate the site it's recommended to stay nearby. Options include **Mom Morokod Koh Ker Guesthouse** (📞078 365656; r US$12) and **Ponloeu Preah Chan Guesthouse** (📞012 489058; Srayong; r US$5), both about 10km from the temples.

✕ **Take a Break**

It's pretty remote here and the only food stalls of note are clustered outside the entrance to Prasat Krahom and Prasat Thom. Most open during daylight hours only and turn out simple dishes.

strangler figs; the probing roots cut through the brickwork like liquid mercury.

An Enigma of a Temple

Koh Ker is one of the least-studied temple areas from the Angkorian period and no restoration work has ever been undertaken here. Louis Delaporte visited in 1880 during his extensive investigations into Angkorian temples. It was surveyed in 1921 by the great Henri Parmentier for an article in the *Bulletin de l'École d'Extrême Orient*. Archaeological surveys were also carried out by Cambodian teams in the 1950s and '60s, but all records vanished during the destruction of the 1970s, helping to preserve this complex as something of an enigma.

Several of the most impressive pieces in the National Museum in Phnom Penh come from Koh Ker, including the huge *garuda* that greets visitors in the entrance hall and a unique carving depicting a pair of wrestling monkey-kings.

Looting at Koh Ker

The looting of statues and carvings from the remote temples of Cambodia has been a major problem for almost half a century, although it is no longer a serious issue at most of the significant sites in the Angkor area. Koh Ker was one of the most heavily affected locations in Cambodia, as it housed a large number of ornate, oversized statues in its many towers and shrines. Starting as early as 1970, and with the advent of the civil war, a sophis-

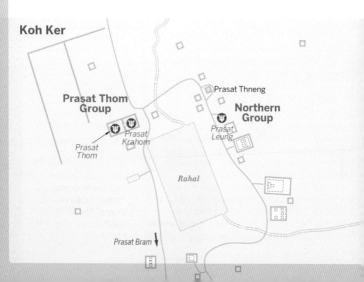

Koh Ker

Prasat Thom Group

Prasat Krahom

Prasat Thom

Prasat Thneng

Northern Group

Prasat Leung

Rahal

Prasat Bram

ticated network of antiquities traders managed to plunder this ancient site of its treasures, with the items crossing the border into Thailand before being sent onwards to auction houses, galleries, private collections and museums around the world. In recent years, the tide has started to turn and a number of museums and auction houses – including the Metropolitan Museum of Art, the Denver Art Museum, Christie's and Sotheby's – have returned prominent pieces to Cambodia that originated in Koh Ker.

Getting There

Koh Ker is 127km northeast of Siem Reap (two hours by car) and 72km west of Tbeng Meanchey (1½ hours). The toll road from Dam Dek, paved only as far as the Preah Vihear Province line, passes by Beng Mealea, 61km southwest of Koh Ker; one-day excursions from Siem Reap often visit both temple complexes. Admission fees are collected at the toll barrier near Beng Mealea if travelling from Siem Reap.

From Siem Reap, hiring a private car for a day trip to Koh Ker costs about US$80. There's no public transport to Koh Ker, although a few minibuses (10,000r) link Srayong, 10km south of Prasat Krahom, with Siem Reap. It might also be possible to take one of the shared taxis that link Siem Reap with Tbeng Meanchey and get off at Srayong.

Top Sight
Beng Mealea

A spectacular sight to behold, Beng Mealea is one of the most mysterious temples at Angkor as nature has well and truly run riot. Built in the 12th century under Suryavarman II to a similar floor plan as Angkor Wat, Beng Mealea is enclosed by a massive moat measuring 1.2km by 900m. Exploring this titan of temples is the ultimate Indiana Jones experience.

បេងមាលា

US$5

🕑 7.30am-5.30pm

The Ultimate Ruin

Beng Mealea used to be utterly consumed by jungle, but some of the dense foliage has been cut back and cleaned up in recent years. Entering from the south, visitors wend their way over piles of finely chiselled sandstone blocks, through long, dark chambers and between hanging vines. The central tower has completely collapsed, but hidden away among the rubble and foliage are several impressive carvings, as well as a well-preserved library in the northeastern quadrant. The temple is a special place and it is worth taking the time to explore it thoroughly.

The large wooden walkway to and around the centre of the temple was originally constructed for the filming of Jean-Jacques Annaud's *Two Brothers* (2004), set in 1920s French Indochina and starring two tiger cubs.

Satellite Temples

Beng Mealea has a large *baray* to the east and some atmospheric satellite temples such as **Prasat Chrey**, which is quite overgrown by jungle and feels like a miniature version of the Beng Mealea of old. Apsara Authority (www.apsaraauthority.gov.kh) has plans to re-flood the ancient *baray*, as they did earlier with Jayatataka (Northern Baray), surrounding Neak Poan temple.

Ancient Angkor Roads

Beng Mealea is at the centre of an ancient Angkorian road connecting Angkor Thom with Prasat Bakan (also known as Preah Khan Kompong Svay) in Preah Vihear Province, now evocatively numbered Route 66. A small Angkorian bridge just west of Chau Srei Vibol temple is the only remaining trace of the old Angkorian road between Beng Mealea and Angkor Thom; between Beng Mealea and Preah Khan there are at least 10 bridges abandoned in the forest. Spean Ta Ong is the most spectacular, a 77m bridge with a

★ **Top Tips**

○ Look out for a mini rendition of the Churning of the Ocean of Milk legend carved onto a fallen lintel near the collapsed central tower of the temple.

○ Head north from Beng Mealea for about 1.5km in the direction of Svay Leu and you will come to a bridge. Stop here and explore the riverbed, as this is the site of an ancient Angkor-era quarry with some chiselled blocks in situ.

✕ **Take a Break**

Several stop-and-sip food stalls (dishes US$2 to US$4) are opposite the temple entrance. Run by friendly, English-speaking Sreymom, the **Sreymom Beng Mealea Homestay** (☏ 087 555229; Beng Mealea Village; r incl meals US$25) is just a short walk away from the temple. Overnight rates include all home-cooked meals; it is possible to pre-arrange lunch here on a visit to Beng Mealea, even if you don't stay.

beautiful *naga*, forgotten in the forest about 28km east of Beng Mealea. This is a way for extreme adventurers to get to Preah Khan temple, but do not undertake this journey lightly.

Day-trip Options

Beng Mealea is about 68km (one hour, US$70 by car; 1½ hours, US$30 by *remork-moto*) from Siem Reap. Allow a half-day to visit, including the journey time from Siem Reap.

In addition to the admission fee there are small charges (ie tolls) for transport, so make sure you work out in advance with the driver or guide who is paying for these. It can be combined with other destinations for a full-day trip, including the remote temple complex of Koh Ker (p126) or the stilted village of Kom-

A Legacy of War

Beng Mealea was only cleared of landmines and unexploded ordnance (UXO) between 2003 and 2007. According to the Cambodian Mine Action Centre (CMAC) sign on the site, 438 anti-personnel landmines were found and 809 pieces of UXO.

pong Khleang (p140) on Tonlé Sap lake. It is even possible to combine it with the main sights in Banteay Srei District, such as Banteay Srei temple (p117), Kbal Spean (p118) (River of a Thousand Lingas) and the Cambodia Landmine Museum (p120), thanks to a useful road link that follows the base of the holy mountain of Phnom Kulen (p122).

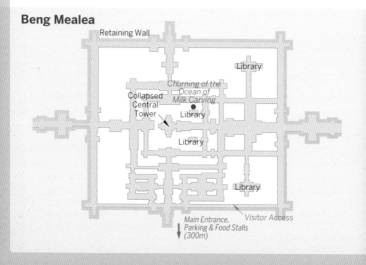

Beng Mealea

Retaining Wall

Library

Churning of the Ocean of Milk Carving

Collapsed Central Tower

Library

Library

Library

Library

Visitor Access

Main Entrance, Parking & Food Stalls (300m)

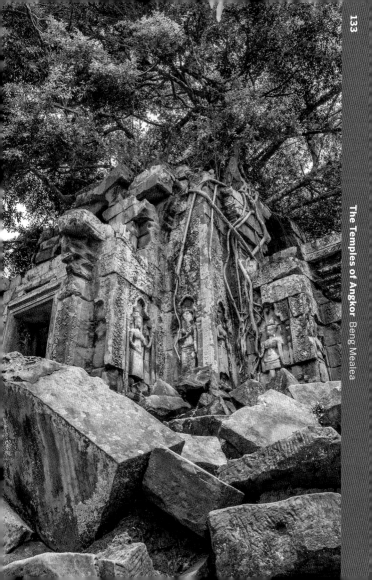

Top Sight 📸
Roluos Temples

The monuments of Roluos served as Indravarman I's capital Hariharalaya. Harihara, who gave his name to the ancient capital. is a unique fusion deity found only in Cambodia, combining attributes of Shiva and Vishnu. The Roluos temples are among the earliest large, permanent temples built by the Khmers and mark the dawn of Khmer classical art. As well as the imposing pyramid temple of Bakong, the Roluos group also includes the brick temples Preah Ko and Lolei.

The temples can be found 13km east of Siem Reap along NH6 near the town of Roluos. A half-day trip from Siem Reap to the Roluos temples by *remork-moto* costs about US$20. You can also reach the temples easily enough by bicycle.

Bakong

The largest and most interesting of the Roluos temples, **Bakong** (បាគង; ⏰7.30am-5.30pm) was built by Indravarman I and dedicated to Shiva. It is a representation of Mt Meru and served as the city's central temple. The east-facing complex consists of a five-tier central pyramid of sandstone, 60m square at the base, flanked by eight towers of brick and sandstone, and other minor sanctuaries. A number of the lower towers are still partly covered by their original plasterwork. Before the construction of Bakong temple, generally only lighter (and less durable) construction materials such as brick were used.

The complex is enclosed by three concentric walls and a moat. There are well-preserved statues of stone elephants on each corner of the first three levels of the central temple. The sanctuary on the fifth level was a later addition during the reign of Suryavarman II, in the style of Angkor Wat's central tower.

There are 12 stupas – three to each side – on the third tier. There is also an active Buddhist monastery here, dating back a century or more.

Preah Ko

Built by Indravarman I in the late 9th century, **Preah Ko** (ព្រះគោ; ⏰7.30am-5.30pm) was dedicated to Shiva. Preah Ko was also dedicated to his deified ancestors in AD 880, the front towers in tribute to male ancestors or gods and the rear towers to female ancestors or goddesses. Lions guard the steps up to the temple.

The six *prasats* (stone halls), aligned in two rows and decorated with carved sandstone and plaster reliefs, face east; the central tower of the front row is a great deal larger than the other towers. Preah Ko has some of the best surviving examples of plasterwork seen at Angkor and is currently under restoration. There are elaborate inscriptions in the ancient Hindu language of Sanskrit on the doorposts of each tower.

★ **Top Tips**

o It's best to start your visit with Lolei, then visit Preah Ko and finish at Bakong, as each structure is architecturally more dramatic than the last.

o Plan a half-day visit together with the stilted village of Kompong Pluk or allow two to three hours to explore the three temples.

o There are some rarely visited temples to the south of the Roluos group, including the atmospheric brick temple of Prei Monti, which you will likely have entirely to yourself.

✕ **Take a Break**

There are a couple of excellent local restaurants in the Prasat Bakong District. **Natural Vegetable Food Place** (meals US$3-7; ⏰9am-9pm) specialises in organic vegetables served with a pungent dip. The sprawling **Stoeng Trorcheak Restaurant** (meals US$3-12; ⏰7am-10pm; ❄ 📶) is set by the Roluos River and offers an eclectic menu.

Lolei

The four brick towers of **Lolei** (លលៃ; ⏱7.30am-5.30pm), an almost exact replica of the towers of Preah Ko (although in much worse shape), were built on an islet in the centre of a large reservoir – now rice fields – by Yasovarman I, the founder of the first city at Angkor. The sandstone carvings in the niches of the temples are worth a look and there are Sanskrit inscriptions on the doorposts. According to one of the inscriptions, the four towers were dedicated by Yasovarman I to his mother, his father and his maternal grandparents on 12 July 893.

Shopping Around the Roluos Temples

Several good-cause initiatives have sprung up around the Roluos area.

Look out for **Prolung Khmer** (www.prolungkhmer.blogspot.com; ⏱8am-5pm) on the road between Preah Ko and Bakong. It's a weaving centre producing stylish cotton *krama* (checked scarves), set up as a training collaboration between Cambodia and Japan.

Right opposite Preah Ko is the **Khmer Group Art of Weaving** (Preah Ko; ⏱7am-5pm), turning out silk and cotton scarves on traditional looms. Also here is **Dy Proeung Master Sculptor** (donations accepted; ⏱6am-6pm), who has created scale replicas of Preah Ko, Bakong and Lolei, plus Angkor Wat, Preah Vihear and Banteay Srei for good measure.

Not far from here on NH67 is the **Lo-Yuyu** (www.loyuyuceramics.com; NH67; ⏱8am-6pm) ceramics workshop, producing traditional Angkorian-style pottery.

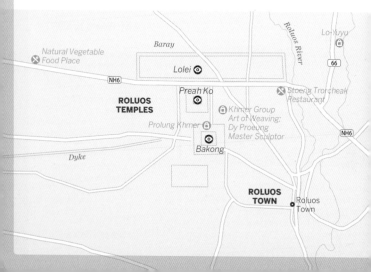

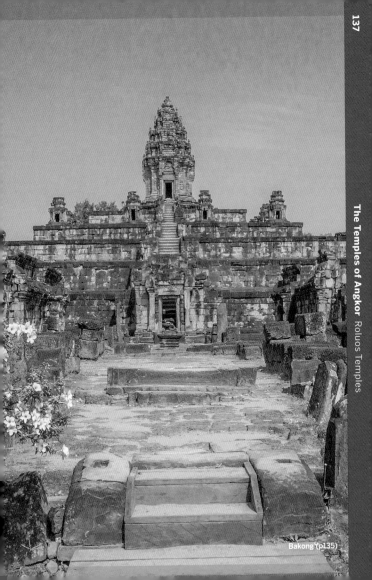

Bakong (p135)

Top Sight 📷
Floating Villages of the Tonlé Sap

The Tonlé Sap may be a miracle of nature, but the floating villages that dot the lake are also out of this world. Whole villages float on the surface of the lake, their livelihoods dependent on the freshwater fish catch. Everything floats in these communities, including the school, the clinic and even the karaoke bar. Other villages are built on immense stilts, like giant bamboo skyscrapers, to ensure they remain above water in the wet season floods.

Distances from Siem Reap to the floating villages vary from 11km to Chong Kneas to more than 50km to Kompong Khleang and Prek Toal. These villages are best accessed by a combination of road (by *moto/remork*/taxi) and boat.

Floating Village of Chong Kneas

The famous **floating village of Chong Kneas** (ភូមិអណ្ដែតទឹកចុងឃ្នាស; boat trip per person US$20, entrance fee US$3) has become somewhat of a circus in recent years. Tour groups have taken over and there are countless scams to separate tourists from their money. That said, for all its flaws, Chong Kneas is very scenic in the warm light of late afternoon and can be combined with a sunset visit to the nearby hilltop temple of Phnom Krom.

To get to Chong Kneas from Siem Reap costs US$3 by *moto* each way (more if the driver waits), or US$15 or so by taxi. The trip takes 20 minutes. Alternatively rent a bicycle in town and just pedal out here, as it is a leisurely 11km through pretty villages and rice fields.

Kompong Pluk

The village of **Kompong Pluk** (កំពង់ភ្លុក; boat trip per person US$20, community fee US$1) is a friendly, otherworldly place where houses are built on soaring stilts about 6m high. Nearby is a flooded forest, inundated every year when the lake rises to take the Mekong's overflow. As the lake drops, the petrified trees are revealed. Exploring this area by wooden dugout in the wet season is very atmospheric. Best visited from July to December, it is not worth the effort in the dry season months of January to June, as litter chokes the earth and there are pungent smells from stagnant ponds of water.

There are a couple of basic homestays in Kompong Pluk and lots of good floating restaurants for lunch or a snack.

The most popular way to get here is by road via the small town of Roluos (about US$10/15/30 by *moto/remork/taxi*) and then boat. All said, the road-and-boat route will take up to two hours, but it depends on the season – sometimes it's more by road, sometimes more by boat. Dry season access time is around one

★ Top Tips

○ Avoid the madding crowds at the floating village of Chong Kneas by asking your boat driver to take some back channels.

○ One of the best ways to visit Chong Kneas is on an all-inclusive trip with **Tara Boat** (☏092 957765; www.taraboat.com; per person incl lunch/dinner US$29/36).

○ Visitors to Chong Kneas should stop at the **Gecko Centre** (www.greengecko project.org; ⊙8.30am-5.30pm), an informative exhibition that helps to unlock the secrets of Tonlé Sap.

○ **Unique Kayak Cambodia** (☏097 456 2000; http://uniquekayakcambodia.com; half-day US$70-115, full day US$100-150) offers kayaking trips to explore the flooded forest near Me Chrey and paddle around the village.

✕ Take a Break

Kompong Pluk has the best selection of restaurants, including floating eateries offering specialities such as fresh baby lake shrimp.

hour. Tara Boat offers day trips here for US$60 per person. The other option is to come via the floating village of Chong Kneas, where a boat (1¼ hours, US$55 return) can be arranged.

Kompong Khleang

One of the largest communities on the Tonlé Sap lake, **Kompong Khleang** (កំពង់ឃ្លាំង; boat trip per person US$11.75-26, entrance fee US$2) is more of a town than the other villages, and comes complete with several ornate pagodas. Most of the houses here are built on towering stilts to allow for a dramatic change in water level. Fewer tourists visit here compared with the floating villages closer to Siem Reap, so that might be a reason to visit in itself. There is only a small floating community on the lake, but the stilted town is an interesting place to browse for an hour or two.

There is a handful of homestays in Kompong Khleang for those that want to stay the night. All are set in imposing stilted houses and there is even a 'boutique' homestay available. There are no real restaurants here, but several food stalls cook up fresh fish and other dishes. Most homestays also provide meals for guests.

Kompong Khleang is not difficult to reach from Siem Reap thanks to an all-weather road via the junction town of Dam Dek. The trip will cost about US$60 return by taxi; it's a long ride by *remork*, but it should cost less (around US$25 to US$30).

Me Chrey

One of the more recently 'discovered' floating villages, **Me Chrey** (មេជ្រៃ; boat trip per person from US$18, entrance fee US$1) moves with the water level and is prettiest during the wet season, when houses are anchored around an island pagoda. It is one of the smaller villages in the area but sees far fewer tourists than busy Chong Kneas.

Me Chrey lies about 25km from Siem Reap on a pretty dirt road that passes through lush rice fields if you happen to be travelling between July and November. Arrange transport by road (about US$10/20/30 for a *moto/remork/*taxi) before switching to a boat to explore the area.

Prek Toal

One of three biospheres on the Tonlé Sap lake, **Prek Toal** (boat trip per boat US$55) is home to a stunning **bird sanctuary** (ជម្រកសត្វស្លាបទឹកព្រែកទាល់; admission US$20; ⊙6am-6pm). It is an ornithologist's fantasy, with a significant number of rare breeds gathered in one small area. Even the uninitiated will be impressed, as these birds have a huge wingspan and build enormous nests.

During the peak season (December to February) visitors will find the concentration of birds like something out of a Hitchcock film. As water starts to dry up elsewhere, the birds congregate here. Rare birds include the spot-billed pelican, milky stork, greater adjutant, black-headed ibis and the secretive

Tonlé Sap: Heartbeat Of Cambodia

Tonlé Sap, the largest freshwater lake in Southeast Asia, is an incredible natural phenomenon that provides fish and irrigation waters for half the population of Cambodia. It is also home to 90,000 people, many of them ethnic Vietnamese, who live in 170 floating villages.

Linking the lake with the Mekong at Phnom Penh is a 100km-long channel known as the Tonlé Sap River. From June to early October, wet-season rains rapidly raise the level of the Mekong, backing up the Tonlé Sap River and causing it to flow northwestward into the Tonlé Sap lake. During this period, the lake surface increases in size by a factor of four or five, from 2500 sq km to 3000 sq km up to 10,000 sq km to 16,000 sq km, and its depth increases from an average of about 2m to more than 10m. In October, as the water level of the Mekong begins to fall, the Tonlé Sap River reverses direction, draining the waters of the lake back into the Mekong.

This extraordinary process makes the Tonlé Sap an ideal habitat for birds, snakes and turtles, as well as one of the world's richest sources of freshwater fish: the flooded forests make for fertile spawning grounds, while the dry season creates ideal conditions for fishing. Every year the Tonlé Sap lake produces about 300,000 tons of fish. Experts believe that fish migrations from the lake help to restock fisheries as far north as China.

This unique ecosystem was declared a Unesco Biosphere Reserve in 2001, but this may not be enough to protect it from the twin threats of upstream dams and rampant deforestation.

masked finfoot. The birds remain beyond February but the sanctuary becomes virtually inaccessible due to low water levels. It is possible to visit from September, but bird numbers may be lower.

Several ecotourism companies in Siem Reap arrange trips out to Prek Toal including the Sam Veasna Center (www.samveasna. org), Osmose (www.osmosetonle sap.net), and Prek Toal Tours & Travel (www.prektoal-tours.com), which is run by Prek Toal villagers. Tours include transport, entrance fees, guides, breakfast, lunch and water. Binoculars are available on request, plus the Sam Veasna Center has spotting scopes that they set up at observation towers within the park. All three outfits can arrange overnight trips for serious enthusiasts. Day trips include a hotel pick-up at around 6am and a return by nightfall.

Survival Guide

Before You Go

Book Your Stay

○ Siem Reap has the best range of accommodation in Cambodia. A vast number of family-run guesthouses (US$5 to US$20 per room) and a growing number of hostels cater for budget travellers. In the midrange, there's a dizzying array of good-value pool-equipped boutiques (US$30 to US$70) with something of a price war breaking out in low season. High-end options abound but don't always offer more than you'd get at the midrange.

○ During the low season (May to early October), there are lots of special offers available ranging from stay three/pay two deals to big discounts in the range of 30% to 50%. Top-end hotels usually publish high- and low-season rates.

○ It's advisable to book ahead from November to March, particularly

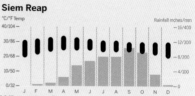

When to Go

Nov–Mar Siem Reap and the temples of Angkor are very busy at peak season, so it rewards to explore further afield.

Apr & May Temperatures hit the 40s, making for some sweaty touring amid a dry and barren landscape.

Jun–Oct The wet season months offer an emerald green landscape and the floating or stilted villages of the Tonlé Sap are at their most colourful.

if you're eyeing one of the glamorous spots, but with more than 600 guesthouses and hotels in town, you won't be without a bed if you just show up.

○ Most hotels will include a free transfer from the airport, bus station or boat dock if you ask, and breakfast is almost always included at the midrange end and up.

○ Many top-end hotels levy an additional 10% government tax, 2% tourist tax, and sometimes an extra 10% for service.

Useful Websites

Lonely Planet (www.lonelyplanet.com/cambodia/siem-reap#lodgings) Reviews of Lonely Planet's top choices.

Siem Reap Beyond the Temples (www.visitsiemreap.com.kh) Community-based tourism website with accommodation listings beyond the town.

Best Budget

Green Home I (www.thegreenhome.org) Set up like a family guesthouse with beautiful garden views.

Onederz Hostel (https://onederz. com) One of the smartest hostels in Siem Reap and winner of several 'Hoscars' (Hostelworld's Oscars).

Mad Monkey (www. madmonkeyhostels. com) Classic backpacker with deluxe dorms.

Seven Candles Guesthouse (www. sevencandlesguest house.com) Profits are used to help a local foundation that seeks to promote education in rural communities.

Siem Reap Hostel (www.thesiemreap hostel.com) Well-tended dorms in Angkor's original backpacker hostel.

Best Midrange

Mulberry Boutique Hotel (www.mulberry-boutiquehotel.com) Generously proportioned rooms decked out with love seats, Jacuzzi-like baths and balconies.

Pavillon Indochine (www.pavillon-indochine.com) Charming colonial-chic rooms set around a small swimming pool.

1920 Hotel (www.1920hotel.com) Budget boutique hotel in a grand old building near Psar Chaa.

Soria Moria Hotel (http://thesoriamo ria.com) Promotes local causes to help the community; half owned by hotel staff.

Steung Siem Reap Hotel (www. steungsiemreap.com) French colonial–style hotel near Psar Chaa.

Best Top End

Phum Baitang (www. zannierhotels.com) Beautiful resort that feels like a boutique Cambodian village.

Sala Lodges (www. salalodges.com) Offers 11 traditional Khmer houses that have been turned into a rustic boutique hotel.

Viroth's Hotel (www. viroth-hotel.com) Ultra-stylish, retro-chic property with 30 rooms fitted out with classy contemporary furnishings.

HanumanAlaya Villa (www.hanumanalaya. com) Boutique hotel with traditional Cambodian stylings.

Shinta Mani (www. shintamani.com) Contemporary chic design by renowned architect Bill Bensley.

Arriving in Siem Reap

Airport

All international flights arrive at the **Siem Reap International Airport** (☎063-962400; www.cambodia-airports. com), 7km west of the town centre. Facilities at the airport include cafes, restaurants, bookshops, international ATMs and money-changing services.

There are no direct flights between Cambodia and the West, so all visitors will end up transiting through an Asian hub such as Bangkok in Thailand; Vientiane, Luang Prabang and Pakse in Laos; Ho Chi Minh City (Saigon),

Hanoi and Danang in Vietnam; Hong Kong; Kuala Lumpur in Malaysia; Beijing, Guangzhou, Kunming and Shanghai in China; Busan and Seoul in South Korea; Singapore; Taipei in Taiwan; and Manila in the Philippines.

Domestic links are currently limited to Phnom Penh and Sihanoukville. Airlines operating domestic flights include Bassaka Air (www.bassakaair.com), Cambodia Angkor Air (www.cambodiaangkorair.com), Cambodia Bayon Airlines (www.bayonairlines.com) and JC International Airlines (www.jcairlines.com). Demand for seats is high during peak season, so book as far in advance as possible.

Many hotels and guesthouses in Siem Reap offer a free airport pick-up service with advance bookings. Official taxis are available next to the terminal for US$9. A trip to the city centre on the back of a *moto* is US$3 or US$7 by *remork-moto*.

Boat

There are daily express boat services between Siem Reap and Phnom Penh (US$35, five to six hours) or Battambang (US$20, four to eight hours or more, depending on the season). The boat to Phnom Penh is rather overpriced these days, given it is just as fast by road and so much cheaper. The Battambang trip is seriously scenic, but breakdowns are *very* common.

Boats from Siem Reap leave from the floating village of Chong Kneas near Phnom Krom, about 11km south of Siem Reap. The boats dock in different places at different times of the year; when the lake recedes in the dry season, both the port and floating village move with it. An all-weather road has improved access around the lake area, but the main road out to the lake takes a pummelling in the annual monsoon.

Most of the guesthouses in town sell boat tickets. Buying the ticket from a guesthouse usually includes a *moto* or minibus ride to the port. Otherwise, a *moto* out there costs about US$3, a *remork* about US$7 and a taxi about US$15.

Bus

All buses depart from the **bus station and taxi park**, which is 3km east of town and nearly 1km south of NH6. Tickets are available at guesthouses, hotels, bus offices, travel agencies and ticket kiosks. Some bus companies send a minibus around to pick up passengers at their place of lodging. Upon arrival in Siem Reap, be prepared for a rugby scrum of eager *moto* drivers when getting off the bus.

Bus companies in Siem Reap:

Asia Van Transfer (AVT; ☎ 063-963853; www.asiavantransfer.com; Hup Guan St) A daily express minivan departs at 8am to Stung Treng (US$20, five hours) via Preah Vihear City (Tbeng

Meanchey), with onward services from Stung Treng to Don Det (Laos), Ban Lung and Kratie.

Capitol Tour (☎ 012 830170; www.capitoltours cambodia.com) Buses to destinations across Cambodia.

Giant Ibis (☎ 095 777809; www.giantibis. com) Has free wi-fi on board.

Golden Bayon Express (☎ 063-966968; https:// bayonvip.com; Wat Bo Rd) Express minivan services to Phnom Penh.

Liang US Express (☎ 092 881183; Sivatha St) Has some direct buses to Kompong Cham.

Mekong Express (☎ 063-963662; https:// catmekongexpress.com; 14 Sivatha St) Upmarket bus company with hostesses and drinks.

Nattakan (☎ 078 795333; Concrete Drain Rd) The first operator, and still one of the most reliable, to do direct trips to Bangkok (US$28, 7½ hours, 8am and 9am). It's out of the way so request a free pick-up.

Neak Krorhorm (☎ 063-964924; Siem Reap River Rd East) Direct buses to Bangkok (US$28, nine hours, 8am and 9am) with no change at the border.

Phnom Penh Sorya (☎ 096 766 6577; https:// ppsoryatransport.com.kh; Sivatha St) Most extensive bus network in Cambodia.

Virak Buntham (☎ 017 790440; www. virakbuntham.com) The night-bus specialist to Phnom Penh and Sihanoukville.

Car & Share Taxi

The new road linking Siem Reap to Phnom Penh is in excellent shape and private cars can now do the journey in four hours, much of that on a divided four-lane highway. The roads west to Sisophon and north to Anlong Veng are also in great condition.

Share taxis and other vehicles operate along some of the main routes and these can be a little quicker than buses. Destinations include Phnom Penh

(US$10, five hours), Kompong Thom (US$5, two hours), Sisophon (US$5, two hours) and Poipet (US$7, three hours). To get to the temple of Banteay Chhmar, head to Sisophon and arrange onward transport there (leave very early).

Getting Around

Bicycle

Some guesthouses around town hire out bicycles, as do a few shops around Psar Chaa, usually for US$1 to US$2 a day.

The **White Bicycles** (www.thewhitebicycles.org; per day US$2) project rents bikes through over 50 guesthouses and hotels in Siem Reap, with all proceeds going towards supporting local development projects around town. Imported mountain bikes are available from cycling tour operators for around US$8 to US$10 per day.

Another option is the wonderful **Green e-bikes** (095 700130; www.greene-bike.com; Central Market; per 24hr US$10; 7.30am-7pm), an environmentally sound compromise between bicycle and motorbike, with three charge points out at the temples and several more in the city. Several additional shops in the centre hire out electric bikes.

Car & Motorcycle

Most hotels and guesthouses can organise car hire for the day, with a going rate of US$30 and up. Upmarket hotels may charge more. Foreigners are technically forbidden to rent motorcycles in and around Siem Reap, but the rules have relaxed and motorbike hire is now widely available. You can now even rent self-drive *remorks* through **Angkor e-Tuk Hostel** (088 824 1919; Siem Reap River Rd East), which has a fleet of powerful, oversized electric *remorks* (per day US$24). You can easily drive these

to outlying temples and back on a single charge.

Moto

A *moto* (unmarked motorcycle taxi) with a driver will cost from US$10 per day depending on the destination. Far-flung temples will involve a higher fee. The average cost for a short trip within town is 2000r or so, and around US$1 or more to places strung out along the roads to Angkor or the airport. It is probably best to negotiate in advance as a lot of drivers have got into the habit of overcharging.

Remork-Moto

Remork-motos are sweet little motorcycles with carriages (commonly called *tuk tuks* around town), and are a nice way for couples to get about Siem Reap, although drivers like to inflate the prices. Trips around town start from US$2, but you'll need to pay more to the edge of town at night. Prices rise when

you add three or more people.

Essential Information

Business Hours

Everything shuts down during the major holidays: Chaul Chnam Khmer (Khmer New Year), P'chum Ben (Festival of the Dead) and Chaul Chnam Chen (Chinese New Year).

Banks 8am to 3.30pm Monday to Friday, Saturday mornings

Bars 5pm to late

Government offices 7.30am to 11.30am and 2pm to 5pm Monday to Friday

Museums Hours vary, but usually open seven days a week

Restaurants (international) 7am to 10pm or meal times

Restaurants (local) 6.30am to 9pm

Shops 8am to 6pm daily

Local markets 6.30am to 5.30pm daily

Discount Cards

Senior travellers and students are not eligible for discounts in Cambodia.

Electricity

Type A
120V/60Hz

Type C
220V/50Hz

Money

Cambodia's currency is the riel, abbreviated in our listings to a lower-case 'r' written after the sum. Cambodia's second currency (some would say its first) is the US dollar, which is accepted everywhere and by everyone, though small amounts of change may arrive in riel.

If multiple currencies seems a little excessive, perhaps it's because the Cambodians are making up for lost time: during the Pol Pot era, the country had *no* currency. The Khmer Rouge abolished money and blew up the National Bank building in Phnom Penh.

The Cambodian riel comes in notes of the following denominations: 100r, 200r, 500r, 1000r, 2000r, 5000r, 10,000r, 20,000r, 50,000r and 100,000r.

The US dollar remains king in Cambodia. Dollar bills with a small tear are unlikely to be accepted by Cambodians, so it's worth scrutinising the change you are given to make sure you don't have bad bills. Pay for something cheap in US dollars and the change comes in riel.

ATMs are widely available in Siem Reap. Credit cards are accepted by many hotels and restaurants. For cash exchanges, markets (usually at jewellery stalls or dedicated money-changing stalls) are faster and less bureaucratic than the banks. Useful banks include:

ABA Bank (Tep Vong St; ⊙ 8.30am-3.30pm Mon-Fri, to 11.30am Sat) Withdrawals are limited to US$100 per transaction and there is a US$4 transaction fee per withdrawal.

ANZ Royal Bank (Achar Mean St; ⊙ 8.30am-3.30pm Mon-Fri, to 11.30am Sat) Does credit-card advances. Several branches and many ATMs (US$5 per withdrawal) around town.

Canadia Bank (Sivatha St; ⊙ 8.30am-3.30pm Mon-Fri, to 11.30am Sat) Offers credit-card cash advances (US$4) and changes travellers cheques in most major currencies at a 2% commission.

Tipping

Tipping is not traditionally expected, but in a country as poor as Cambodia, tips can go a long way.

Hotels Not expected outside the fanciest hotels, but 2000r to US$1 per bag plus a small tip for the cleaner will be a nice surprise.

Restaurants A few thousand riel at local restaurants will suffice; at fancier restaurants you might leave 10% on a small bill, 5% on a big bill.

Remorks & Moto Drivers Not expected for short trips, but leave a dollar or two for half-day or full-day rentals if the service was noteworthy.

Temples Most wats have contribution boxes – drop a few thousand riel in at the end of a visit, especially if a monk has shown you around.

Service Charges Many of the upmarket hotels levy a 10% service charge, but this doesn't always make it to the staff.

Public Holidays

Banks, ministries and embassies close down during public holidays and festivals, so plan ahead if visiting Cambodia during these times. Cambodians also roll over holidays if they fall on a weekend and take a day or two extra during major festivals. Add to this the fact that they take a holiday for international days here and there, and it soon becomes apparent that Cambodia has more public holidays than any other nation on earth!

International New Year's Day 1 January

Victory over the Genocide 7 January

International Women's Day 8 March

International Workers' Day 1 May

International Children's Day 8 May

King's Birthday 13–15 May

King Mother's Birthday 18 June

Constitution Day 24 September

Commemoration Day 15 October

Independence Day 9 November

International Human Rights Day 10 December

Safe Travel

o Cambodia is a pretty safe country for travellers these days, with few incidences of petty crime.

o Remember the golden rule: stick to marked paths in remote areas (due to the possible presence of landmines).

o *Phnom Penh Post* (www.phnompenhpost.com) is a good source for breaking news, so check its website before you hit the road to check the political pulse and catch up with any recent events on the ground such as demonstrations.

o Take care with some of the electrical wiring in guesthouses, as it can be pretty amateurish.

Toilets

Cambodian toilets are mostly of the sit-down 'throne' variety. The

Dos & Don'ts

The Cambodian people are very gracious hosts, but there are some important spiritual and social conventions to observe.

Buddhism When visiting temples, cover up to the knees and elbows, and remove your shoes and any head covering when entering temple buildings. Sit with your feet tucked behind you to avoid pointing them at Buddha images. It's also good to leave a small donation. Women should never touch a monk or his belongings.

Meet & Greet Called the *sompiah*, the local greeting in Cambodia involves putting your hands together in a prayer-like manner. Use this when introduced to new Khmer friends. When beckoning someone over, always wave towards yourself with the palm down.

Modesty Avoid wearing swimsuits or scanty clothing around towns in Cambodia, even in beach destinations. Wear a sarong to cover up.

Saving face Never get into an argument with a Khmer person. It's better to smile through any conflict.

occasional squat toilet turns up in homestays or budget guesthouses and out the back of provincial restaurants.

The issue of toilets and what to do with used toilet paper is a cause for concern. Generally, if there's a wastepaper basket next to the toilet, that is where the toilet paper goes, as many sewerage systems cannot handle toilet paper. Toilet paper is seldom provided in the toilets at bus stations or in other public buildings, so keep a stash with you at all times.

Many Western-style toilets also have a hose spray in the bathroom, aptly named the 'bum gun' by some. Think of this as a flexible bidet, used for cleaning and ablutions as well as hosing down the loo.

Public toilets are rare, the exception being some beautiful wooden structures dotted about the temples of Angkor. The charge is usually 500r for a public toilet, although they are free at Angkor on presentation of a temple pass. Most petrol stations have some sort of toilet.

Should you find nature calling in remote border areas, don't let modesty drive you into the bushes: there may be landmines not far from the road or track. Stay on the roadside and do the deed, or grin and bear it until the next town.

Tourist Information

Check out *Siem Reap Pocket Guide* (www.cambodiapocketguide.com) for the low-down on restaurants, bars, shops and services, widely available in town. The *Siem Reap Angkor Visitors Guide* (www.canbypublications.com) is packed with listings and comes out quarterly.

ConCERT (www.concertcambodia.org) Works to build bridges between tourists and good-cause projects in the Siem Reap/Angkor area, with information offices at Sister Srey Cafe (p54) and New Leaf Book Cafe (p55). It offers information on anything from ecotourism initiatives to volunteering opportunities.

Siem Reap Tourism Office (☎ 063-959600; Royal Gardens) A large new office is under construction in the Royal Gardens; it may become a useful stop in the future.

Travellers with Disabilities

Broken pavements, potholed roads and stairs as steep as ladders at Angkor ensure that for most people with mobility impairments, Siem Reap and the temples of Angkor will not be easy places to travel. At Angkor Wat and the other temples of the area, causeways are uneven, obstacles common and staircases daunting, even for able-bodied people. It is likely to be some years before things improve, although some ramping is now being introduced at major temples.

In Siem Reap, few buildings have been designed with accessibility in mind, although the airport and most top-end hotels include ramps and lifts for wheelchair access. Most guesthouses and small hotels have ground-floor rooms that are reasonably easy to access.

On the positive side, the Cambodian people are usually very helpful towards all foreigners, and local labour is cheap if you need someone to accompany you at all times. Wheelchair travellers will need to undertake a lot of research before visiting Siem Reap.

Visas

o A one-month tourist visa costs US$30 on arrival and easily extendable business visas are available for US$35. Most nationalities receive this on arrival at Phnom Penh, Siem Reap or Sihanoukville airports, and at land borders. One passport-sized photo is required and you'll be 'fined' US$2 if you don't have one. It is also possible to arrange a visa through Cambodian embassies overseas or to get an online e-visa (US$30, plus a US$7 processing fee) through the Ministry of Foreign Affairs (www.mfaic.gov.kh).

o Passport holders from ASEAN member countries do not require a visa to visit Cambodia.

o Travellers are sometimes overcharged when crossing at land borders with Thailand, as immigration officials demand payment in baht and round up the figure considerably.

o Overstaying a visa currently costs US$5 a day.

Language

The Khmer language is spoken by approximately nine million people in Cambodia, and is understood by many in neighbouring countries. Although Khmer as spoken in Phnom Penh is generally intelligible to Khmers nationwide, there are several distinct dialects in other parts of the country. In Siem Reap there's a Lao-sounding lilt to the local speech – some vowels are modified, eg *poan* (thousand) becomes *peuan*, and *kh'sia* (pipe) becomes *kh'seua*.

The pronunciation guides in this chapter are designed for basic communication rather than linguistic perfection. Read them as if they were English, and you shouldn't have problems being understood. Some consonant combinations are separated with an apostrophe for ease of pronunciation, eg 'j-r' in *j'rook* (pig) and 'ch-ng' in *ch'ngain* (delicious). Also note that *k* is pronounced as the 'g' in 'go'; *kh* as the 'k' in 'kind'; *p* as the final 'p' in 'puppy'; *ph* as the 'p' in 'pond' (hard and rolling); *t* as the 't' in 'stand'; and *th* as the 't' in 'two'. Vowels and vowel combinations with an *h* at the end are pronounced with a puff of air at the end.

To enhance your trip with a phrasebook, visit lonelyplanet. com. Lonely Planet iPhone phrasebooks are available through the Apple App store.

Basics

Hello.	ជម្រាបសួរ	*johm riab sua*
Goodbye.	លាសិនហើយ	*lia suhn hao-y*
Yes.	បាទ/ចាស	*baat/jaa* (m/f)
No.	ទេ	*te*
Please.	សូម	*sohm*
Thank you.	អរគុណ	*aw kohn*
You're welcome.	អត់អីទេ/ សូមអញ្ជើញ	

awt ei te/ sohm onh-jernh

Excuse me./ Sorry.

សូមទោស *sohm toh*

How are you?

អ្នកសុខសប្បាយទេ? *niak sohk sabaay te*

I'm fine.

ខ្ញុំសុខសប្បាយ *kh'nyohm sohk sabaay*

Does anyone speak English?

ទីនេះមានអ្នកចេះ *tii nih mian niak jeh*
ភាសាអង់គ្លេសទេ? *phiasaa awngle te*

I don't understand.

ខ្ញុំមិនយល់ទេ/ *kh'nyohm muhn yuhl te/*
ខ្ញុំស្ដាប់មិនបាន *kh'nyohm s'dap muhn baan te*

Eating & Drinking

Where's a ...?

...នៅឯណា? *... neuv ai naa*

food stall

កន្លែងលក់ ម្ហូប *kuhnlaing loak m'howp*

market	ផ្សារ	psar
restaurant		
ភោជនីយដ្ឋាន		resturawn

Do you have a menu in English?

មានម៉ឺនុយជា
ភាសាអង់គ្លេសទេ?

*mien menui jea
piasaa awnglay te*

What's the speciality here?

ទីនេះមានអ្វី
អ៉ីពិសេសទេ?

*tii nih mien m'howp
ei piseh te*

I'm vegetarian.

ខ្ញុំតមសាច់   *kh'nyohm tawm sait*

I'm allergic to (peanuts).

កុំដាក់ (សណ្តែកដី)   *kohm dak
(sandaik dei)*

Not too spicy, please.

សូមកុំធ្វើហ៊ឺរពេក

*sohm kohm
twœ huhl pek*

This is delicious.

អានេះឆ្ងាញ់ណាស់   *nih ch'ngain nah*

The bill, please.

សូមគិតលុយ   *sohm kuht lui*

Emergencies

Help!

ជួយខ្ញុំផង!   *juay kh'nyohm phawng*

Call the police!

ជួយហៅប៉ូលិសមក!   *juay hav police mok*

Call a doctor!

ជួយហៅ
គ្រូពេទ្យមក!

*juay hav
kruu paet mok*

I've been robbed.

ខ្ញុំត្រូវចោរប្លន់

*kh'nyohm treuv
jao plawn*

I'm ill.

ខ្ញុំឈឺ   *kh'nyohm cheu*

I'm allergic to (antibiotics).

ខ្ញុំមិនត្រូវធាតុ
ថ្នាំ
(អង់ទីប៊ីយ៉ូទិក)

*kh'nyohm muhn
treuv thiat
(awntiibiowtik)*

Where are the toilets?

បង្គន់នៅឯណា?

*bawngkohn neuv
ai naa*

Transport & Directions

Where is a/the ...?

...នៅឯណា?   *... neuv ai naa*

How can I get to ...?

ផ្លូវណាទៅ...?   *phleuv naa teuv ...*

Where's the ...?

...នៅឯណា?   *... neuv ai naa*

  airport

  វាលយន្ត ហោះ   *wial yohn hawh*

  bus stop

  ចំណត ឡានឈ្នួល   *jamnawt laan
ch'nual*

  train station

  ស្ថានីយ រថភ្លើង   *s'thaanii roht plœng*

When does the ... leave?

...ចេញម៉ោង
ប៉ុន្មាន?

*... jeinh maong
pohnmaan*

boat	ទូក	duk
bus	ឡានឈ្នួល	laan ch'nual
train	រថភ្លើង	roht plœng
plane	យន្តហោះ	yohn hawh

Index

See also separate subindexes for:

- ⊗ Eating p156
- ⊙ Drinking p157
- ⊗ Entertainment p158
- ⊙ Shopping p158

Sights 000
Map Pages 000

Behind the Scenes

Send Us Your Feedback

We love to hear from travellers – your comments help make our books better. We read every word, and we guarantee that your feedback goes straight to the authors. Visit **lonelyplanet.com/contact** to submit your updates and suggestions.

Note: We may edit, reproduce and incorporate your comments in Lonely Planet products such as guidebooks, websites and digital products, so let us know if you don't want your comments reproduced or your name acknowledged. For a copy of our privacy policy visit lonelyplanet.com/privacy.

Nick's Thanks

A huge and heartfelt thanks to the people of Cambodia, whose warmth and humour, stoicism and spirit make it such a fascinating place to live. Biggest thanks are reserved for my lovely wife, Kulikar Sotho, and our children, Julian and Belle, as without their support and encouragement the adventures would not be possible. Thanks also to Mum and Dad for giving me a taste for travel from a young age.

Thanks to fellow travellers and residents, friends and contacts in Cambodia who have helped shaped my knowledge and experience in this country. There is no room to thank everyone, but you all know who you are. Finally, thanks to the Lonely Planet team who have worked on this title.

Acknowledgements

Cover photograph: Angkor Wat, Martin Puddy/Getty Images ©

Photographs pp24–5 (from left): Pelikh Alexey/Shutterstock ©; Mark Read/Lonely Planet ©; Martin Puddy/Getty Images ©

This Book

This 3rd edition of Lonely Planet's *Pocket Siem Reap & the Temples of Angkor* guidebook was curated, researched and written by Nick Ray. This guidebook was produced by the following:

Destination Editor
Laura Crawford

Series Designer
Campbell McKenzie

Cartographic Series Designer Wayne Murphy

Senior Product Editor
Kate Chapman

Product Editor
Kathryn Rowan

Senior Cartographer
Diana Von Holdt

Book Designer
Lauren Egan

Assisting Editors Victoria Harrison, Gabrielle Innes, Mao Monkolransey, Tamara Sheward

Cartographer Anita Banh

Cover Researcher
Brendan Dempsey-Spencer

Thanks to Hannah Cartmel, Liz Heynes, Virginia Moreno, Martine Power, Rachel Rawling

Our Writer

Nick Ray

A Londoner of sorts, Nick comes from Watford, the sort of town that makes you want to travel. He studied history and politics at Warwick University before hitting the road for a life in travel and has worked on about 50 titles for Lonely Planet since his first foray in 1998. Based in Cambodia, he covers countries in Southeast Asia, including Cambodia, Laos, Myanmar and Vietnam, with the occasional diversion to Africa. Aside from Lonely Planet, Nick also works as a location scout and line producer for film and television, including everything from *Tomb Raider* to *Top Gear*.

Published by Lonely Planet Global Limited
CRN 554153
3rd edition – Oct 2018
ISBN 978 1 78701 264 6
© Lonely Planet 2018 Photographs © as indicated 2018
10 9 8 7 6 5 4 3 2 1
Printed in Singapore

Although the authors and Lonely Planet have taken all reasonable care in preparing this book, we make no warranty about the accuracy or completeness of its content and, to the maximum extent permitted, disclaim all liability arising from its use.